All the best

Amanda Blackburn

"*Finally*, there's an entertaining and intriguing book on personal sales for thinking people, written by someone who really gets it!"
— Tea Hoffman, Esq. — Author of:
THE PROACTIVE PRACTICE

I have practiced law for thirty-two years and, before that, was in sales for ten years. In my opinion, Chuck Blackburn has explored the depths and nuances of the art of sales in a fresh and exciting manner. Read, study, learn and apply his lessons if you wish for success in personal sales.—**George M. Johnson, P.C.**

STOP SELLING! ...LET 'EM BUY is easy to read, informative, and has plenty of good humor. It's filled with inspirational quotes, and reading it is like sitting down with a seasoned sales professional over a cup of coffee while he shares his heart about a profession he clearly loves. Chuck Blackburn is a gifted communicator who will inform, enlighten, and inspire you whether you're reading his book or have the pleasure of hearing him speak.
The book changed the way I think about selling. I loved reading this book!
—Martha Bolton—Emmy nominated writer for Bob Hope (15 years) and the author of over 50 books of humor, including **DIDN'T MY SKIN USED TO FIT?** and **COOKING WITH HOT FLASHES**

Dedication

This book is dedicated to my wife, Marsha Blackburn—my love and my inspiration. She is the hardest working person I have ever known. And her leadership is aptly displayed in her new book—
Life Equity (www.yourlifeequity.com)
I once quipped about Marsha, "A woman's place is in the House–and in the Senate!" (She was State Senator when I made that remark)

> "Samson killed a *thousand* Philistines with the jawbone of an ass. That many sales are killed every day using the *same weapon!*"
> –Anonymous

Smart sales principles, tactics, and strategies

STOP SELLING!
...Let 'em Buy

A Rare Collection of Time Tested Techniques from Forty Years of Extraordinary Sales Experience

By Chuck Blackburn

"If you always do what you've always done, you'll always get what you've always got"
 –Anonymous

"Learn something new every day??? Why not every minute? Why limit ourselves? Can we ever *really* know enough?"
–Me

Why?
Why another sales book? What distinguishes *this* one? What gives it any sort of *unique value*? Why would you invest your time and resources and give multiple copies to colleagues, employees, clients, friends, and family?

There is a singular premise that separates this book from the rest…

It is written expressly for those who believe there is *more* to sales—possibly *much* more—than common knowledge and past experience dictates.

This book challenges common sales practices and offers positive alternatives to stereotypical sales methods. It utilizes quotes, anecdotes, and personal experiences to drive home the central message.

Everything we *think* we know about sales should periodically be questioned and validated so it can be improved upon (the profession is *fraught* with flawed and outdated premises)

Most of us *want* to believe we know enough. The notion of additional training can be disturbing. This is especially true if you view yourself as an accomplished and experienced top producer. Isn't that the implication as well as the predicament? Do you really need to be having problems or experiencing weakness to seek external information? Let me ask you this…Do you wait for your car to bellow smoke before you change the oil?

And what's the old adage about an *ounce of prevention*? "If it ain't broke, don't fix it"…doesn't mean it can't be maintained and improved upon! Right?

If you can't sell; this book won't be much help. Its three-fold bottom line value for those desiring to stay on top of their game is:
- Validation of what you *already know* so you'll use it *more* with increased confidence, enthusiasm, and results.
- As a reminder of previously effective ideas you just might have inadvertently gotten away from over time that, if redeployed, will work surprisingly well.
- An introduction to *one* or *two* innovative thoughts that, if they fit your personality and your industry (and work!), you'll use them *over and over again* to reach heights never before imagined!

Change Happens
Bygone are the days of *adversarial* relationships between salespeople and prospects pitting *you-against-them*. Remember hearing, "The first person that talks loses"?

Even longer past is the "show up and throw up" mentality while wishing and hoping for sales. The "trick 'em and stick 'em" stereotype never works in the long run.

The popular *make a friend and hope they buy* results in few sales and even fewer friends.

Please don't take this wrong. However, if you *just* want a friend–rescue a dog from the pound. If you want to proactively *help* people you can more likely do so by continuously improving your sales skills, proficiency, self motivational, and organization habits to better manage your time, and–dare I say it–increase your Federal tax liability and your discretionary income!

Rapidly changing times and markets require more progressive; more *evolutionary* and creative approaches to personal sales. It's time to *stop selling and let 'em buy*!

In other words–don't give them what they *expect*. Stop acting in a manner which prospects are accustomed. As a positive alternative–actively lend a hand to qualified prospects in defining their own needs– emotionally evoke a clear understanding of the benefits and values you offer– then…shut up and close at the first sign of interest!

Now, would you like some good news?
You don't need to work twice as hard or stress twice as much to double your sales. There are many good notions to help you simply work *smarter*.

If you really want to improve sales proficiency–for yourself and/or your salespeople–herein are some encouraging words and powerful ammunition to help you along the way.

I have borrowed and drawn from both my own experience and from many of today's top producers in an attempt to impact you so you may better enjoy the game of sales.

If you've ever battled the voices in your head that say, "I already know enough" or "I can't do any better" here are hundreds of thoughts and ideas proven as an antidote to this poisonous, counterproductive thinking.

Again, understand and consider every idea and explanation herein–select one or two–discover what fits–then use them over and over again thousands of times to make hundreds of thousands you would *not* have made if you hadn't opened your mind to go through with the exercise.

All this will guarantee that you sell *more* in considerably *less* time serving *more* people, earning *more* money, and better enjoying your job and possibly even adding more overall balance to your life!

> **"The primary object of education is not about gaining knowledge or wisdom– but about *action*. It is not what you know but what you remember to use that gets the job done."**
> **–Anonymous**

Irrevocable truth…
It may sound elementary, however, it's not only *what* you know; it's what you *do* with what you know and how and when you do it.

> "You are better than you think you are, but you are not as good as you want to be"
> –Anonymous

Contents

Preface

Introduction: Before You Begin

1 My Personal Experience

2 Fanciful History—5000 BC

3 Will History Repeat Itself...? Again?

4 Basic Premises

5 Fundamental Building Blocks

6 May I Ask You A Question?

7 Forget the Beef. Where's the Sizzle?

8 What is the Unpardonable Sin?

9 Call Reluctance, Fear of Rejection and Failure, and Emotional Hurdles

10 Third Parties Make the World Go Round

11 Not Listening, Not Hearing

12 Drivers Drive, Thinkers Think, and Buyers Buy

13 Disparities between What's Sold and What's Delivered

14 Prospects, References, Referrals

15 Reaching Decision Makers

16 The Simple Genius

17 Wrench the Heart without Wrinkling the Shirt

18 The Red Herring Dilemma

19 Elevator Statements and Networking

20 Communicating Clear Value Propositions (VP)

21 Goals, Planning, Accountability, and the Law of Averages

22 The 800-Pound Gorilla

23 Why Don't All Interested Prospects Buy?

Preface

There are no shortcuts to experience. I should know–I have spent my entire professional life desperately seeking the proverbial path of least resistance.

In a larger sense, if experience is the quintessential *teacher*— doesn't it follow that extraordinary experience over an extended timeframe results in exceptional education?

I have always been a great proponent that life can either be a dynamic learning experience or a frustrating series of missed opportunities.

Keeping this in mind, it me took forty years of professional successes and failures to log enough first-hand experience and vicarious learning to complete this book. Happily, it won't take anywhere near that much time for you to digest.

This work addresses the role of personal sales psychology, principles, practices, strategy, and innovation for personal growth and business success. It is not at all intended to be one of those "how-to books for *dummies*".

Nor does it claim to be a collection of in-your-face sales tips, tricks, secrets, killer questions, or sure-fire gimmicks. It is intended to be a positive alternative to the high pressure/ low integrity stereotypes. All of which are of short-lived value and dubious worth.

It is, instead, a comprehensive work for smart, hardworking, *thinking* people. My objective is to put into new perspective that which you may already know. There are no silver bullets and no road to Damascus miracles promised or to be expected.

My desire is to expose the value of what *you don't know you don't know* about the art and the science of personal selling. Please re-read that last sentence aloud. Does it make sense that there is more you do not know than you know? How much do you need to know? Can you ever know enough?

This is especially the case for techniques and strategies that defy conventional wisdom and weather the storms of trial and error.

I reiterate, the ideas, tools, and tactics herein include–but are not limited to– *my personal practice*. The concepts, methods, and initiatives have been tested over decades by a host of diverse sales personalities in a myriad of different industries, products, and services.

There are no knee-jerk or rush-to-judgment theories proffered here. I consider such notions intellectually dishonest and insulting to thinking people who understand and appreciate the quest for *genuine value*.

This collection of ideas is meant for individuals who *get it* and companies that *need it*. The "it" I refer to holds special relevance for firms finally coming to recognize that personal sales talent and execution are essential weapons in their competitive arsenal. Additionally, this book is intended to take some of the mystery out of effective sales practices.

It is my long held belief there is an urgent need in our business community to recognize the power of "above average" sales *wisdom*. This especially holds true for sales practices and techniques demonstrating the highest ethical standards.

The Purpose
Clarity is the objective. My primary goal is to convey unambiguous insights into the in and out's of applied personal sales strategy and technique in a rapidly changing and increasingly competitive world.

The mission is to shed overdue light on the whys-and-wherefores behind personal sales style and execution. As previously mentioned–most of this is achieved by way of a very hands-on approach.

Insuring that members within an organization are properly *sold on sales* produces both short term and continuous benefits for those participating.

There are a host of valid yet less obvious reasons for all members in an organization to better understand the art and principles of personal sales expertise, motivation, technique, and strategy.

These very same principles have also proven valuable in the functions of purchasing, managing sales, and managing people.

Ironic (or at least *paradoxical*)
Popular career fields requiring graduate studies like *product development* and *product management* necessitate much more than just a tacit knowledge and understanding of professional sales acumen. MBA students seeking entrée into business upon graduation are frequently *required* to participate for two years in outside sales prerequisite to these positions. It's amusing to envision a newly-minted MBA's chagrin as he or she suddenly recognizes this requirement and responds, "I didn't get an MBA to be a lowly salesperson!"

It is my long-held belief that everyone is *in* sales, more or less, everyday. This is true in our professional as well as our personal lives.

The same sales and persuasion philosophies and principles are fundamental to activities including: parenting, leadership, teaching, coaching, politics, law, religion, interviewing, conflict resolution, socializing, or encouraging a friend.

Again *what* is this book...what is it good for?
I hope you will employ this book as a handy reference, a training manual, or a valuable guide to increased understanding and proficiency in personal sales. (There are some *other* options including doorstop, paperweight, or credenza decoration.)
As always, it is your own personal choice–so please chose wisely.

Remember, it's impossible to know what we don't know. My experience has been that the more I learn, the more I realize there *is* to learn. I wish I had humbled myself to listen a lot earlier.

"You should learn from the mistakes of others. We don't have time to make them all ourselves."
–Groucho Marx

Introduction:

I might say "before you begin"; however by now you realize you are *already* well on your way!

This is a test--an intellectual exercise…
Try to be honest with yourself. Realize the unrelenting battle between what you want to believe and what is probable. See what you may not want to see. Now ask yourself:

"Would *you* buy from you? *Would* you buy from you? Now the 'hat trick': *Why* would you buy from you?"

Note the subtle change in meaning when you voice this curious query putting the emphasis on different words.

Now, why ask these similar-yet-different somewhat rhetorical questions? Getting you to think purposefully about the reality of sales is my transparent motive.

Setting the stage with unconventional questions should cause you to:
- Ponder whether the value of what *you*–the seller offers fits the needs and resources of *you*–the prospective buyer
- Disregard the obvious vested interest, perfect knowledge, and perfect mobility (everyone in the *you–you* relationship *knows* and has unencumbered access to everything you offer)
- Think about what motivations or tendencies you may or may not know about yourself as a seller or a prospective buyer
- Consider that you–the seller–may have a different personality than you–the buyer.

You meet you…
You–the salesperson, only have one thing in common with you–the prospect: That is the awareness that you are trying to sell to you. Yet you do not necessarily want to be sold by *anyone*…not even *you!*

All this despite you–the prospect–may want or need that which you–the salesperson–are selling. Of course, you may just be in the mood to buy–or maybe not.

Stay with me
Now that you have the basic assumptions established in your mind, let's revisit the pivotal question from yet a fourth perspective. Would you really buy from *you*, *your* company, or *your* employees?

Moreover, would you be satisfied afterward? How enthusiastically would you recommend others follow suit?

I know this is a bit of an intellectual conundrum. All the same I can assure you the game will be worth the mental gymnastics. You will find it only takes a little effort and an active imagination to play. Let's hope you're up to it. Besides–it will be fun.

Now trust your instincts while suspending your inhibitions. And please don't let up on the intellectual aerobics. By remaining engaged you gain momentum. You *do* believe in revelations…don't you?

The Questions to Ask Yourself
How would you prepare to sell to you? What would you do to induce yourself to make this complicated sales transaction with you–the prospective buyer–move forward?

First step
- How would you motivate yourself to begin?
- How would you overcome call reluctance
- How would you overcome your fear of rejection?
- How would you make initial contact with you?
- Where would you get pre-approach information you need?
- What information will you require about you?

Prospecting
- How would you learn you existed?
- Who would you learn this from?

Initial contact
- When and how would you make initial contact with you?
- How would you go about working with your receptionist or your gatekeeper?

Qualifying
- What questions would you ask you to gain confidence, rapport, and credibility?
- What would you ask to set the tone for the presentation, avoid objections, and set up the close?

The presentation
- Can you effectively and efficiently obtain your attention, create ample interest and evoke emotional desire?
- How long should the presentation be?
- When and how would you trial close?

The close
- How and when would you consummate the deal with action?
- Is immediate action appropriate?
- Can you assume you are the final decision maker?
- What kind of close would be most appropriate?
- How would you trial close?
- Will your value proposition be compelling enough to close?

Handling objections
- Could you handle your objections?
- Which are real and which are excuses?

Follow-up
- If getting to a decision requires subsequent meetings how would you set them up and make sure they happen?
- How would you get the decision influencers together and accountable?

A glimmer at the end of the tunnel

As a lifelong ardent student of sales, I've observed that survival, much less growth of any organization requires an unmitigated "yes" at least thirty-three percent of the time to every variation of the inquiry, and "Would you buy from you?"

Additionally, it is vital that the most prolific of producers constantly pursue excellence in all of the above under all conditions and in all circumstances.

Directly, these dogmatic assertions only hold credence in competitive landscapes. You know you are *always* in competition with someone—even if only with yourself. When one tiny voice in your head says, "I can't", the louder voice interrupts, "I can, I will, I'm going to!"

> **"The three great essentials to achieving anything worthwhile are first, hard work, second, stick-to-it-iveness, and third, common sense."**
> **—Thomas A. Edison**

You can do more than you think
We all possess the ability to out-dream, out-create, out-think, out-smart, out-plan, as well as out-work, the smartest people in the world. This is the great poetic justice we enjoy by living and competing in our great free enterprise system.

Challenge
These *exercises* in improvement are for those of you who are better than you think but not quite as good as you want to be.

So I must ask: "Do you have resolve to take steps today—right now—to follow your imagination? Really, do you really have the resolve?"

A life-long student of selling— I have read and reread hundreds of books and articles on personal sales.

I did this not only to learn; but to validate what I know from my own experience. I also continue to pick up anything that might help me improve. You never know what ideas you're going to find in sales books. Some, but not all, are even worthwhile!

I never take anything written about sales as gospel. I try it, internalize it, teach it…but only if it works long term, and I observe other sales personalities utilizing it. I have found that many seemingly great ideas on the surface do not work consistently in the real world.

The better you understand proven sales principles, the more people you will be able to serve and the more you'll appreciate the art of the influence of personal sales.

I delighted in the idea of coaching and mentoring hundreds of outstanding sales people in action on the field. As a result, everything I know has been twice, or even thrice, learned.

All instruction came about while using live ammo and dodging real bullets. I also paid meticulous attention to what could be learned from every school-of-hard-knocks experience. I read assiduously while taking copious, and I might add, exhaustive notes along the way.

The principles outlined throughout this writing are based upon a lifetime of extensive personal sales experience both business-to-business (B2B) as well as business-to-consumer (B2C). Most of my experience has been in outside sales. Once more, the ideas, concepts, and suggestions were conceived directly from an abundance of field-proven successes and embarrassing yet enlightening bumps and slumps.

It is my heartfelt wish that when you pick up this book you find the techniques, experiences, and observations interesting, hopefully insightful, and sometimes amusing, while instructive to your personal sales education.

You can always do better

Each of us has the opportunity to improve our performance. And it doesn't require going back to school to learn new skills. It doesn't even require brushing up on the where-fores, why-nots, and how-tos of your business.

What it does take is someone who will evaluate your work honestly and carefully each day.

Someone who will tell you that your performance on a project was good – but not good enough

Who is that person? *You* are that person!

CHAPTER ONE
Personal Experience

> "It is tough to admit it but when I was eighteen I thought I knew more than I did." –Me

I ran away from home on a typical hot June day in Fort Worth, Texas. The year was 1966 and I had just turned seventeen.

I took a job selling Fuller Brush products door-to-door. Yes, I was a teenage *Fuller Brush Man!* (A good country song title, you think?)

To say the least, this new endeavor was horrifying, especially at that tender age. I immediately began to discover deep-seated life lessons from this traumatic first-hand experience. Fear of failure was always with me (little did I know that it would become my greatest motivator throughout life.)

I was the quintessential "newbie". I poured over the Fuller product samples, training materials, prices, closes, and answers to objections. Virtually every sales and business term was foreign to me. It was confidence I lacked, confidence I needed and confidence I finally got.

"Whatever you do, you need courage. Whatever course you decide upon there is always someone to tell you that you are wrong. There are always difficulties arising which tempt you to believe that your critics are right. To map out a course of action and follow it to the end requires some of the same courage which a soldier needs."
—Emerson

It quickly became apparent that the act of confronting my personal demons door-to-door would be the foremost means of building genuine self-confidence. This personal revelation was an unanticipated consequence of rather naïve actions. I was literally running scared between houses all that summer as I distributed samples of *free* hand lotion and took orders for Fuller Brush cleaners, sprays, and, of course, brushes.

No mortal could have been more surprised than I was when virtually overnight I became the top salesperson in the entire east Fort Worth district. It might as well have been the entire galaxy, as far as I was concerned. I was hooked on sales forever. Looking back through "experience goggles" I thought I understood however I had no idea why I was blessed with that initial success.

That summer I began to study sales with an insatiable desire to never cease learning. I had serendipitously found my life's calling. I had left my comfort zone far behind forevermore.

Question…Could a confirmed introvert become a risk-taking extrovert in just one summer? At age seventeen I learned it definitively *could* happen. It changed my life forever. It led me to the famous Southwestern Company.

Selling books door-to-door
A world-renowned sales training organization, Southwestern Company is located in Nashville, Tennessee.

You may be curious about the name "Southwestern" until you know the company began in 1855 when Tennessee was more a part of the southwest than the southeast United States.

The company was best known for its intense, exceptionally comprehensive sales training and mentoring program for college students. It can be said Southwestern took the least likely sales candidates, trained them, and challenged them in one of the most difficult sales jobs on earth…door-to-door sales.

Over 150 years over 100,000 students voluntarily left home to seek the adventure of working in this summer sales intern program. They all bought into the promise that learning to better communicate ideas and motivate others to act upon those ideas would differentiate them from the crowd. They could not have been more correct.

Southwestern's sales program continues to recruit thousands of college students from all over the world to begin their education in sales. The students learn about themselves and about people through selling books and educational materials door-to-door during their summer vacations.

Throughout history people who accomplished much, including entrepreneurs, business leaders, publishers, lawyers, doctors, judges, civic and church leaders, governors, and members of Congress, occupied their summers working with Southwestern learning some of life's harsher lessons along with many positive experiences.

My relationship with Southwestern
A short time after my Fuller Brush eye-opener, I enrolled at University of Texas - Arlington as a pre-med student.

Around that time, a close friend, Bruce Casburn, introduced me to Southwestern by setting up an interview with Jim Samuel. Jim is a truly great man destined to leave an indelible impression on me forever.

Jim and Bruce teamed up on me and a couple of friends.

It was persuasively extolled on us the benefits of the company's summer sales program. They explained how selling books door-to-door with their training and mentoring would be the very best way ever to earn good money and learn just of what we are made. They said all we needed to do was to, "work hard, study hard, and follow suggestions." Could it be *that* simple? It seemed simple at the time. I *wanted* to believe.

Jim and Bruce assured us regardless of the individual career path we chose there was no better place to gain self-discipline and the skills we needed to succeed in life.

They spoke in grandiose terms about the valuable lessons we would learn while dealing with all kinds of people in a variety of diverse and adverse circumstances.

Jim and Bruce tried valiantly to relate to me all the character building experiences I would have through this ordeal. Quite honestly, I personally had no idea what "character" was all about. "Character" was *not* a term I had ever used in a sentence outside of referring to an animated cartoon character. I did however; understand *m-o-n-e-y*.

They further explained the value of living far away from home for the summer working 80-hour weeks selling books. They neglected to inform me that those eighty hours were actually 81 ½ hours and included only the actual field *selling* time (a small detail).

The hours did not take into account travel, recordkeeping, and continuing sales training. They did let us know the compensation would be straight commission with no guarantees, no draws, and naturally, with us bearing all our own expenses.

I personally knew no other method by which salespeople could be compensated. I was *that* green. By this time I was eighteen years old and convinced I knew it all!

My friends and I were informed that a *relatively* small percentage of the beginning sales people did not make it past the second week on the field (I later learned "relatively" meant twenty to thirty percent).

I figured those "quitters" obviously didn't have what it takes. Jim and Bruce were good at appealing to and challenging my competitive nature by stating, "If you plan on quitting, don't sign up in the first place."

This personal affront didn't scare me at all. To the contrary, the challenge *inspired* me. Yes, it inspired me since only a year before I had unwittingly discovered that *fear of failure* was my foremost personal motivator.

I didn't know for sure about the others…but I knew that I could *never* quit. I had too much to prove and way too much to lose.

This "opportunity" fit me like a golf glove on a Texas sultry summer day.

My dream was to become one of the most accomplished salespeople *ever*. In my heart I knew that *selling* was my gift from the Almighty. I sincerely believed I was obligated to use this special aptitude to positively affect everything and everyone within my sphere on influence. I *wanted* to believe and *live* my dream.

You might say, "I had at least sipped the Kool-Aid" (so to speak)

In retrospect, I knew I had a slight advantage because of my previous summer with Fuller brush. Having this "head start" I had an opportunity and a responsibility to exploit it. Besides, how could I resist? It was predestined. After all, I'm Presbyterian!

During those years selling books I recruited my brother, my friends, their friends, my fraternity brothers, and anyone else I could infect with my undaunted belief in selling.

These *victims* of my enthusiasm believed in what I said. They came with me from Texas all the way to Nashville for training. After formal training we went as a team onto the field of battle like a scene from the movie *Gladiator*. We lived and worked together for the next thirteen weeks.

My responsibility was largely to lead my charges by example. I mentored, managed, and coached them as best I could.

Most of my recruits succeeded while a few fell short. However, *all* of them learned literally *priceless* life lessons. Nobody ever complained about the value of the training or the experience. (Maybe they had some of that grape Kool-aid as well?!?)

Unlike my subsequent sales experiences, Southwestern's door-to-door program was strictly a one-call close transaction. One-call literally meant the sales cycle was twenty minutes—thirty times a day. There were more de facto approaches, presentations, set-ups, trial closes, closes, handling objections, and potential rejection than most professional sales people experience in an average decade. There is no hype—do the math!

In retrospect, placing conservative fair market value, this type of personal sales regimen would be easily many thousands of dollars.

Seasoned sales insiders say that they view the Southwestern training regime to be unavailable *anywhere* at *any price*. The process does not mirror any normal practices in the real business world.

I drew credibility initially from my performance on the book field
This may come off as an unmitigated lack of humility, but my high water mark with Southwestern was having the honor of being the top overall student salesperson in 1972, a year that saw 7200 over-achieving baby boomer collegians competing on the book field.

Looking back, that summer turned out to be Southwestern's biggest ever in the summer sales program. I received the largest commission check in the history of the company to that date. I delivered $40,000 in books and saved over $15,000 in three months, making 800 individual sales, at a time when all transactions were cash-on-delivery and the dollar was worth 6 times what it is today. (*New* cars were $4000, gas 30 cents per gallon, tuition $1500, and text books around $20 each!)
Am I starting to sound like my dearly departed father, or what?

Sales records are made to be broken and those numbers have been obliterated many times by many kids since that time. The top salespeople at Southwestern today can and do *save* well over $50,000 for the summer.

I knew I was extremely blessed and thankful to God. While the money was important, the experience would prove to be absolutely priceless throughout the ensuing years.

I saw the light and changed my major from premed to economics and marketing. I began to entertain the idea of a career in sales.

What differentiated my sales experience most was that I seemed to have inexplicable insights into the reason *why* different prospects bought and why different salespeople were better able to sell. Naturally, discerning how different personalities buy is beneficial to understanding and teaching sales tactics and strategies.

Throughout the years in the book business I was given the opportunity to write or co-author all of my three thousand person division's sales presentations. Additionally, in collaboration with a very creative guy named Joe Martin, we re-wrote the entire company's delivery sales materials. I trained thousands from the stage and hundreds on the field.

The next challenge (opportunity) was to find a way to exploit these hard fought tools of the trade.

After leaving Southwestern in 1978, I sought more demanding, challenging, relationship and conceptual selling situations. There were almost limitless opportunities for people with a proven track record motivated by fear of failure desiring to follow their dreams.

The world needed to buy what the world needed to buy. The only question remained was, "How much and how fast and who would sell it"?

In retrospect
It has been over forty years since knocking on that first door with Fuller Brush in Fort Worth in 1966.

I have been fortunate enough to continue learning while achieving sales records in several different industries. Along the way I've had the opportunity to help thousands succeed in their sales careers. I launched a manufacturers' representative business, worked in the insurance trade, and incubated a number of start-ups and turn-a-rounds primarily in the financial services industry. I have had a hand in introducing and perfecting creative strategies that have built and enhanced successful sales cultures for firms across the country. I discovered a passion for *doing* and *teaching!*

My training style is based on a distinctive implement, test, and revise model. Professional coaching, reporting, accountability, and field motivational support are turning out to be the backbone my success. I teach what I use and I use what works today. Furthermore, everything espouse here is based on the time tested fundamentals.

An ordinary person can do extraordinary things
I possess no unique personality traits, no head-turning good looks, or characteristics that would distinguish me from the next guy. I am the epitome of average in every way with all commensurate insecurities and propensities. I grew up relatively smart, slightly dyslexic, somewhat athletic, and occasionally humorous.

I am a true believer, a sports lover, and a Boy Scout. My dad was a Texas Aggie electrical engineer who taught me by example the value of a strong work ethic (the Great Depression and WWII taught him).

Anyone who ever looked at me or knows me would immediately conclude, "If *he* can do it, I can certainly do it… maybe better."

All things considered, I reiterate (for emphasis) that I count myself inexplicably lucky and extraordinarily blessed.

I learned that it is not what you know but what you remember to use that gets any job done. Moreover, it is also how often and how proficiently you practice these skills that separate you from the average sales producer and order-taker of the world. The *slight edge* (the little thing) makes all the difference. Learning and using that *one nugget* every now and then creates the competitive advantage that can make a *huge* difference.

Sales— just as in medicine, law, politics, et al is only considered *professional* when performed in a professional manner.

> **"Societies that acclaim philosophers as *professional* because they teach philosophy, and disparage plumbers as *unprofessional* for getting their hands dirty neither have theories *nor pipes* that hold water!"**
> **—Dr. Kenneth McFarland**

Frankly, most plumbers I know make more than most philosophers.

Summary: You can learn much from actual experience as well as vicariously, from other peoples' successes and failures. May you never confuse what you learn vicariously with what you discover from actual performance in a situation where your livelihood is in the balance? The two are not mutually exclusive and can be easily confused.

Personal Review: Would *you* buy from you? *Would* you buy from you? Would you *buy* from you? *Why* would you buy from *you*? What are some lessons you have learned from personal experience that were contrary to what you thought you knew from reading, watching, and listening to others?

Notes:

"This makes sense—this works—I can totally do this!"
—Anyone

CHAPTER TWO
Fanciful History 5000 BC

Please do not consider the following imaginary history to be in any way blasphemous. It is not my purpose to in any way offend true believers. Using more than just a little imagination, I will proceed to draw far-fetched conclusions using a story straight from the first book of the Bible.

This made-up story is intended purely to entertain and add drama to illustrate a point. Unencumbered by fact; this story is unabashedly chocked full of *poetic license*. Disclaimers notwithstanding, here goes.

It all started with, well… once upon a time; a long, long time ago
How could anyone have possibly known that since the very beginning of time, the power and influence of personal selling could have been, well, *underestimated*?

In the book Genesis we find something one might be astounded to learn. Naturally, since this is a book on sales techniques and motivation, this story follows suit.

The question with no answer
Did the Creator of heavens and earth choose merely to inform Adam in a somewhat cavalier fashion of the impending doom that would be wrought on mankind if he disobeyed?

Why didn't God persuade, that is, *sell*, Adam on the dire ramifications of eating fruit from the tree of knowledge of good and evil? Why didn't God use His omnipotent powers to convince Adam and Eve of all the positives they could have had? For example, how about freely and shamelessly running naked in the Garden of Eden without a care in the world for all of eternity? Would that be so bad? Wouldn't it be totally better than the negative alternatives?

The downside for this blatant disobedience was that women would experience excruciating pain giving birth and all mankind would forever endure sickness, wars, bureaucracies, and death!

Dare we draw some logical conclusions here?
If logic follows, we can draw only one conclusion. Adam's job was the *first* sales job. His initial assignment was to persuade Eve, the first prospective buyer. After all, nothing was written about God talking to Eve directly to warn her of this little caveat regarding one damn apple tree.

God had to have delegated the sales function of the known universe without investing even one shekel in training, stone tablet flip charts or sales coaching. All of which would have greatly aided Adam in convincing Eve of the downside of a singular bad deal.

Wouldn't the benefits of owning all the trees on the planet have been an easier concept to sell? It seems like original sin could have been easily avoided with the original *no-brainer*!

The nagging question remains: Did the Almighty believe for a minute Adam and Eve understood that were they sold on the meaning of losing it all and suffering death? God is omniscient. He knew everything past and future. Why didn't he prepare Eve emotionally and intellectually for her ill fated meeting with Satan? Isn't this what we are left to believe? (Please remember: this is still tongue-in-cheek. After all, this is a sales book.)

How did Satan do it? Did he make the first sale ever? What was his personal sales strategy and techniques?
First, after researching his limited database, Satan chose his prospect very carefully. He observed that Eve was not convinced as to why she should resist him or the forbidden fruit.

Satan utilized a compelling story in the form of a provocative question, combined with a timely close. He was positive, confident, and above all, brief. He anticipated the predictable objection and turned it into a plausible benefit, even using a trial close question to drive his point home.

Satan's execution was simple and brilliant. He never hesitated to close at the first and always best opportunity. He saw the opening and used the power of personal sales to ruin a perfect existence for all of us, forever. Now that is a powerful influence—however misguided!

Good sales—bad sales
If Satan had been a benevolent salesperson he could have easily convinced the first couple to build a fence around that ill-fated tree. Better yet, he could have sold them a nice lightning bolt to strike down the tree?

Of course he was the only bid and he was without character references. Nonetheless, Adam and Eve were great prospects for anything Satan wanted to sell them. They had no debt and controlled all the assets in the world.

What can we learn?
Were Satan's motives wrong? It goes without saying that his every intention was absolutely dead wrong. That is hardly the point here.

Satan misused the power of personal sales when no one on earth had attended even the most rudimentary training seminar on sales and motivation. It makes one wonder. Adam had literally *everything*. What if he had invested a little time and attention learning basic ethical sales tools and tactics instead of spending valuable time naming all the plants and animals?

Adam could have become a proficient salesperson and given the devil some much-needed competition. After all, Adam had a closer relationship with Eve, the only prospect on earth. I understand they were seeing a great deal of each other. Literally everything in the world would have been completely different, wouldn't it?

And who said selling wasn't important?

Adam and Eve were the first people to encounter an opportunity cost, the most miscalculated waste from *not knowing* what history clearly confirms. Tragically, the first couple learned the hard way. What we do not know can definitely hurt us. It can even kill us.

This is what life was like before sales training.

Summary: The moral of this story is this: Even if you are omnipotent and omniscient and business is good you cannot underestimate the power of a singular personal sales call or the value of a good sales rep.

Personal Review: Would *you* buy from you? Why *would* you buy from you? Would you *buy* from you? Would you buy from *you*? How transparent are your motives? Can you be successful and happy taking advantage of others? If you can fool all the people some of the time and some of the people all of the time don't you only end by fooling yourself?

Notes: _____

_____
_____
_____
_____
_____
_____

"This makes sense—this works—I can totally do this!" —Anyone

CHAPTER THREE
Will History Repeat Itself... Again?

Professionalism and personal sales
Do you ever wonder why so many otherwise intelligent, well-educated, successful people look down their noses on personal sales as a profession?

Who put the negative in stereotype? Why is Willie Lowman in *Death of a Salesman* held up as the consummate stereotype?

Could it possibly be that most of us are exposed to negative sales experiences early in life? Is it something our parents said? Could it be the statement, "They are just trying to sell you" is virtually always used as a derogatory indictment?

Sometimes people praise an outstanding sales figure by saying, "You could sell refrigerators to Eskimos." What are they implying? Like everyone else, Eskimos buy refrigerators so why would friends possibly think it a compliment to proffer this statement?

Isn't it really an insult to the art and the profession of personal sales? How many people believe deep down that the average salesperson is a pushy, presumptuous, insensitive, charlatan just out to fool us and take our time and money?

Could it be the salespeople they were exposed to utilize the wrong tools and tactics in an imprudent way with improper motives? Unfortunately, these misguided amateurs pretending to be salespeople don't know what they don't know and are susceptible to whatever new and improved sales idea they hear loudest.

Unprofessional salespeople are often vulnerable to what I call sales "malarkey", a technical word for tricks and gimmicks designed to hoodwink unknowing prospects. These ideas can be found in many sales books on the shelves today.

There are many self-proclaimed experts with much too little successful field-tested experience praying on the ignorance of the unknowing.

When the blind lead the blind how can one know the other guy is blind?

There is a real hunger for authentic strategies and techniques that perform effectively and efficiently in the long term. Your challenge is to find the right information to satisfy your individual appetite.

> **"If you stand for nothing, you will fall for anything" —Benjamin Franklin**

Like Adam in the Garden of Eden as previously noted aren't we all in sales to a greater or lesser degree? Wasn't it that way even in the beginning? Maybe my fanciful historical twist on the creation story from the Bible was not entirely ridiculous or farfetched after all.

> "What you *do* speaks so loudly, I cannot hear what you say."
> —Ralph Waldo Emerson

Belief in Sales
Do you, or the companies of which you are part, act as if you are sold on sales? Let's scrutinize and be honest. Be a little bit skeptical and ask yourself, "Are the members of senior management paying lip-service or are they giving personal sales its due?"

Based on the actions companies exhibit toward their sales departments, is senior management really sold on the role of sales as an integral part of their organization's long-term success or is personal sales just a necessary and temporary means to a essential end?

How great a role does professionalism and excellence in personal sales play in your firm's overall ongoing business plan?

For example, when sales increase, are members of senior management likely to increase sales compensation or do they view commission percentages and sales bonus payouts as an expendable drain on the bottom line?

Is "sell" a four-letter word in practice in your company?

Here is a dirty little secret that is an undeniable *red flag*:

If unit sales are *not* increasing, everything else your company has worked for can deteriorate in short order.

As costs of doing business increase and competition mounts, attrition becomes a growing problem. Losing valued clients can inevitably wipe out momentum.

Momentum is inexorably coupled with overall employee morale. The result may easily cause a good company to take a decidedly southern route.

Flat sales are the symptom, not the root cause. A major challenge is for organizations to discover first the real reason for what might be one of several problems with their sales effort. Often a new "set of eyes" can and should be employed to drill down to the origin.

Observations of sales performance on the road by means of interactive training can be an effective method toward unearthing exact causes. In other words, companies must locate the correct origin before drawing conclusions and designing a resolution.

Too many companies spend fortunes by diving headlong into trial and error. This most often results on the alteration of everything from sales staff, compensation plans, product mix, sales management, and/or sales training just ending up badly and more often than not losing ground to competitors.

One-size-fits-all solutions in the form of cookie-cutter sales training programs are pervasive in the United States. There are over ten thousand plus referenced on the Internet.

Conventional wisdom more often comes from convenient sounding solutions. Knee-jerk is by far the most prevalent reaction to profit declines.

With the negative turn in unit sales almost everyone in the sales department tends toward panic mode. Defense mechanisms rise up as sales people do whatever necessary to preserve their egos and protect their means of feeding their families.

Blame-game
The resulting blame-game is tantamount to pouring gasoline on a fire. More often, fixing the blame takes precedence over fixing the problem.

The horror stories of previously successful businesses with great ideas imploding greatly outnumber long-term successes. Denying or ignoring the problem only drives the company further from the correction.

Recall from the story recounted in The Book of Genesis. Upon returning to the garden God found Adam and Eve hiding in the bushes ashamed of what they had done. Upon realizing that God knew what they had done, Adam did the manly thing. He immediately blamed Eve. Eve, in turn, blamed Satan. Satan was then relegated to crawling on his belly and eating dust for eternity.

Satan was simply a motivated evil road rep doing his job. He used his apparently good-enough personal sales skills and adequate motivation with impunity.

This demonstrates that personal sales proficiency is truly a two-edged sword. It also confirms that simply showing up and being "good enough" has always been…well "good enough."

Until the real problems are properly defined there can be scant chance of shaping real solutions. Experience-based solutions present a challenge and an opportunity.

Summary: Selling begins with being sold on selling and sold on what you are selling. Additionally, it is dependent upon being genuinely convinced the company standing behind the product/service can perform and deliver as promised. Your reputation is at stake.

Personal Review: Would **you** buy from you? **Would** you buy from you? Why would you **buy** from you? Would you buy from **you**? What if your company wasn't totally behind your personal sales effort? Would you become a loyal long-term customer? Would you enthusiastically volunteer referrals?

Would it just be a matter of time before the house-of-cards imploded?

Notes:
___

"This makes sense—this works—I can totally do this"
—Anyone

CHAPTER FOUR
Basic Premises

Let's start with three basics
I define "premise" as a truthful supposition validated by all available evidence over ample time. I use the word as a synonym for "truth."

There are three such super premises or paradigms fundamental to the enjoyment of, and excelling in, personal sales. Every word throughout this work is predicated upon these principles. Here they are.

Premise I – *"People love to buy as much as they hate to be sold."*
Take a moment to consider the possibility that you may not totally agree with this controversial paradox.

It is not at all my intention to try to convince you to buy something you may not want to buy on your own volition in your own time frame. That would smack of hypocrisy, wouldn't it?

Most of us, upon being confronted by a salesperson, have an overriding thought screaming within our skulls:

"What is it this person really wants from me? Why is he bothering me?"

What if the salesperson's attitude communicates that he is there to help? A salesperson can communicate:
- "My focus is solely on your needs."
- "I can help you get what *you* really want or need."
- "I can help you achieve your goals and realize your dreams."
- "I can help you to get from where you are, to where you most want to be."

What would your response be if you were the prospect? Would your resistance to any clear proposal be counterintuitive?

Enlightened self-interest is a quintessential human condition. It is embedded in your DNA. You can't deny it, and you can't resist it. You can't help it. For heaven's sake—you don't *want* to help it!

Conversely, if the non-verbal signal coming across from the so-called "salesperson" in name only is, "I need to make this sale no matter what. I'll say anything, promise anything, or do anything not to lose this sale!" a different, far less stellar, dynamic occurs.

This negative vibe occurs much all too frequently among average and below average producers. It is indicative of their internalized training and motivation or lack thereof. There is no redeeming long-term value coming from this type of overt self-interest.

It holds true that two different people can go about doing the same thing in identical manners using similar tools while holding contrary motives.

These individuals may employ similar methods and skills and indeed achieve identical short-range results.

However the one exemplifying the purer motive finds the undertaking less demanding and more enjoyable with greater rewards in the long run. Do you need to be reminded that we all live in the long run?

Are you inferring there are selfish reasons for being above reproach in selling? Bingo!

Know what you are talking about. Otherwise, you don't know what you are talking about (and you lose credibility and respect)

Yes, you must know your product or service inside and out. One would think that a given.

Knowing as much as possible about the competition is also more than just a good idea.

I am always perplexed at the baleful misunderstandings, misinformation, and *disinformation* purveyed publicly to the masses regarding the disciplines of business and economics.

How can there be so much information with so little understanding?

Media talking heads aside, we do not make our livings in a "zero-sum" economy. We do not all battle over a finite amount of dollars.

Bill Gates earning billions takes nothing from you or me. His innovative thinking and hard work creates more wealth and opportunity for everyone willing to work hard and smart.

Furthermore, when you help others achieve their goals and dreams it only adds to your success and happiness, both directly and indirectly.

Premise II – "The best personal sales professionals do not *sell*. Instead, they help prospects make timely buying decisions."
Is this really so novel an assertion? I think not. I contend the most effective, efficient, productive, and profitable, known as E2/P2, sales people succeed because they are proficient at helping prospects acquire what they (the prospects) desire.

Yes, this is a different perspective or spin. But when you give it sufficient thought it does make perfect sense, doesn't it?

If not, please try to keep an open mind. Skepticism has its place, but not in regard to this particular issue. The truth here is indubitable and axiomatic. It is so.

If you take this concept to heart wouldn't it imply that greater proficiencies in sales depend increasingly upon the sales pro's passion to serve? Of course it does!

Premise III – "Sales strategies vary constantly. They change with different people at different times in different situations."

These variances depend upon:
- **Type of industry**
- **Growth phases**
- **Product mix**
- **Competitive issues**
- **Micro and macro economics**

The only constant among these is change. This being so, doesn't it follow that maintaining consistent business growth demands constant change, frequent paradigm shifts, and unanticipated detours?

The change culture in which we live is as inevitable as political corruption. Even so, acceptance of this certainty can be problematic for most. There always has been and there always will be some disparity between what is true and what we want to believe.

You enjoy the comfort of the status quo don't you? We all do.

> **"It is not the strongest of the species that survive, nor the most intelligent, but the most responsive to change."**
> **—Charles Darwin**

Art?
In personal selling we can, and do, literally alter meaning and context in mid- sentence and on the fly.

How else do we efficiently introduce new thoughts, products, concepts, services, and ideals to a dynamically diversifying society?

The essence of the art of personal selling, properly deployed, is the most steadfast and trustworthy source for the information rich, direct, and immediate feedback. There never will be and there never has been a more effective system of market research to show you if people will actually buy.

Will the dog eat the dog food? That is a question to which you can quickly find a definitive answer. The best way to execute this market research is to place the food in the bowl near the dog and then observe what happens.

The role of personal sales in business growth
Personal selling is a major component in creating business growth. Most would readily agree that selling represents the fuel, the gas and oil creating opportunity allowing our free economy system to function.

You may take for granted—at your own peril—that everyone in your organization has a precise understanding and appreciation for the role of personal selling.

It can be counterproductive for anyone in a marketing or sales business, from clerk to chairman, to even passively harbor small misconceptions or misunderstandings about the role of personal sales excellence to business growth.

Isn't everyone's livelihood within the firm directly dependent upon the by-product of effective, efficient personal sales success? Don't all businesses share an unambiguous choice, that is, to grow or die?

> **"By definition, selling is the ability to effectively communicate ideas and motivate others to act upon those ideas."**
> **—Earl Nightingale**

Nothing happens in business unless or until something is sold. Nothing good happens unless more and more satisfied customers buy over and over while referring their friends.

The ultimate interaction
Personal selling is actually a sub-set of the general universe of marketing. Marketing puts emphasis primarily on product while selling is more about the prospective customer.

Most marketing does not directly involve personal selling. Personal selling is not defined as the mass repetition of a particular message repeatedly exposed in the same manner toward different people.

De facto—you can say nothing can be "marketed" unless or until it has first been *sold* to someone along the way.

Selling puts exacting emphasis on finding and understanding the needs, perceptions, and motivations of individual prospects.

The personal interchange of ideas and feelings is a primary distinguisher between personal sales and other forms of marketing.

A personal sale is differentiated by the dynamic interaction between buyer and seller. This personal contact presumes the prospect is not necessarily motivated or even educated with a propensity to buy. It is, for the most part, what has to happen prior to the commoditization of any idea. If it doesn't sell, can it be successfully marketed? Interesting question…

Products must be sold before they can be marketed.

It would be intellectually dishonest, as well as somewhat naïve, to conceive that the value of microwave ovens, cell phones, and Gore-Tex® could exist without the applied excellence of professional selling.

Sales and other forms of marketing are not mutually exclusive. Marketing and personal sales are designed to complement, not compete, with one another.

Summary: What then, is your ultimate objective? Is it to truly help others succeed? Your service attitude will always stand out in a world filled with exploitation.

It is impossible to know what you don't know. You don't know it simply because you don't know it. Nevertheless you can never lose an insatiable thirst for knowledge. The paradox here is the less we know; the more we think we know. The more we know; the more we realize we need to know. We live life on a need-to-know basis and we determine what we need to know. Know what I mean?

Personal Review: Would **you** buy from you? **Would** you buy from you? Would you **buy** from you? Would you buy from **you**? I challenge you to answer this question relative to the insights gleaned from each topic in this chapter. This exercise may help you capture morsels of new information you may then practice, command, internalize, and call your own.

Notes:

"This makes sense—this works—I can totally do this!"
—Anyone

CHAPTER FIVE
Fundamental Building Blocks

The power of three
There are three and only three things anyone in sales can do to increase production.
- See *more* prospects
- See *better* prospects
- Make *better* sales presentations

Four phases within seven steps
Basic to personal selling, or any communications for that matter, includes four phases (AIDA; **A**ttention, **I**nterest, **D**esire, **A**ction):

- *Getting Attention.* Without it, who listens? Personal sales is an interactive dialogue
- *Creating Interest.* Finding and addressing the W.I.I.F.M. or what's in it for me?
- *Arousing Desire.* Decisions are made emotionally and justified intellectually. Passion triumphs over facts and stats.
- *Evoking Action.* Isn't closing the primary goal of selling? Without decisions we are only politely conversing with no objective in mind.

The seven basic steps of every sale are:

- **Prospecting and referrals.** Personal selling differs from mass marketing in that you must find the best prospects to target.
- **Pre-approach.** It is not uncommon to invest two hours preparing for a twenty-minute prospect sales call.
- **Initial Contact.** Use the pre-approach information to set-up the presentation meeting.
- **Set-up or rapport.** Qualifying, questioning, and probing. Emotionally connecting or engaging prior to the presentation shows how much you care about the person rather than the sale.
- **Presentation or demo.** Describing and tailoring the features and benefits are now tailored to the prospects needs and motivations.
- **Trial Close and Close** .Trial closing determines if you can ask for the business thus leading naturally and seamlessly into asking for the business.
- **Consideration** (paperwork/pay). There is no business (for long anyway) without written agreements and/or payment.

Objections

Objections (not to be confused with "excuses) are often considered one of the steps in the overall cycle. However they may occur during *any* or all phases and/or steps of the sale. Handling objections, as a subset of every part will be addressed in some detail later on (Chapter 18).

Some things are more obvious than others. Yes, you should attend to what needs to be done to hold attention, no more or less.

In the same vein, once an individual step is accomplished, either pre-existing or proactively generated, it is imperative to proceed immediately and seamlessly forward to maintain momentum. Don't oversell.

Drill

It is a great exercise and essential planning to write, rewrite, revise, and memorize word-for-word all seven steps of the sale using greatest economy and simplicity of words.

I am not suggesting that anyone recite every word memorized in any given sale. That's canned speech. Most every effective demo is tailored and punctuated by trial close questions. They are tuned in to the interests of the prospect.

Effective memorization is transparent and never appears stilted sounding mechanical.

Impromptu presentations often exceed the prospect's attention span. Rambling and/or deletion of vital features or benefits can result.

You must know precisely where you are, where you've been, and where you are going in the memorized presentation. Always think and observe, and always be brief.

Summary: Being aware of the basic building block construction helps us to appreciate the function.

Personal Review: Would *you* buy from you? *Would* you buy from you? Would you *buy* from you? Would you buy from *you*? Be honest with yourself. How well have you mastered the building blocks of the sale? Do you believe in memorizing all parts of the presentation?

Sure, memorization is a stressful and laborious undertaking however it is well worth it. You will always be glad you did.
Make it fun. Use a mirror.

Notes:

"This makes sense—this works—I can totally do this!"
—Anyone

CHAPTER SIX
May I Ask You a Question?

Is the question the answer?
You can't ask a question until you know something, which requires asking questions. This will be demonstrated here with an overuse of the questioning technique. Need I say (ask) more?

How important is the right kind of question asked the right way? Wouldn't it be a critical success factor?

Am I right or am I wrong? Take this as a rhetorical to make a point.

Questions about questions:
When is the best time to ask a question in a sales presentation?
What are the best questions to ask?
What are the wrong questions and the wrong times to ask questions?
Is there a particular manner in which you ask different kinds of questions before, during, or at the end of a presentation?

What questions get attention, engage thinking, gather information, show interest, set the tone, define the agenda, maintain focus, test interest or understanding, close, smoke out or answer objections?

Types of questions:
Rhetorical questions have played important roles throughout literary history.
"What's in a name? Can a rose by any other name smell as sweet?"
"What made you so smart?"
"To be or not to be" (Perhaps *the* rhetorical question)
"What if we could save money and make money at the same time?"
"Why not be proactive rather than reactive?"
"Et tu, Brute?"

Should one really answer a rhetorical question?
Rhetorical questions are not meant to be answered. Sometimes waiting for an answer can create confusion and pressure. Rhetorical questions are used to make a statement, point out the obvious, get you to think, get attention, and/or maintain focus. They are, however, also useful in setting up an obligating question sometimes referred to as a "tie down" question.

Tie Down Question

Examples:
"That makes sense, doesn't it?"
"You see how that works, don't you"
"That's a no-brainer, isn't it?"

As long as prospects are not engaged, they cannot buy. When prospects are not thinking, they cannot become engaged and they will not buy.

When used properly, rhetorical questions can get attention, interest, desire or all three.

> **"Our greatest sales enemy is not the competition. It is prospect indifference."**
> —Anonymous

When are the best times to ask questions?
In light of what you're trying to accomplish, isn't that an elementary question, dear Watson? What is your intention? Aren't you trying to help people buy? Or are you just educating people about your product/service? Are you just talking *at* people or with people?

If you are steadfastly focused on engaging prospects, shouldn't you turn virtually everything into some sort of question? Could you? Should you?

Can statements be used as questions?
"Let me ask you a question" is not a question at all. It is a declarative statement used purely as an attention getter.

Without attention, there is no dialogue. Without dialogue, there is no understanding. Without understanding, there can be no communication. You can guess the rest.

Questions maintain control
Isn't this non-question a good way to get things back on track? Yes, because a real question or a statement can follow it.
Example (gently interrupting): "By the way, before I forget, just out of curiosity, may I ask you this?"

Prefix/Suffix
Properly prefixing and/or suffixing questions can both open minds and reduce the possibility of pressure to keep things on track.

Examples: Prefix: "Just out of curiosity…
        Suffix: "…even if only for future reference."
        "…anyway, just a thought."

Probing questions
These questions play a major role in gathering information and setting the tone.

"Probing" is somewhat a misnomer. The better verbal description would be "engaging" questions. The content of these questions and manner in which you ask them is indicative of your genuine interest in helping the prospect if, in fact, you truly are interested in the prospect's desires.

Examples:
    "At this point in your business growth, which is more important; decreasing costs or increasing business?"
    "What new initiatives are you presently implementing to do that?"
    "How is that working for you?"

Trial Close Questions:
This is used to maintain attention and test interest. It is a way to stick in your toe before taking the plunge.
Examples:
    "Are you with me so far?"
    "Are you following me?"
    "Does that make sense?"
    "Does that sound fair?"

Caution: Trial close questions are *not* obligating questions. Therefore, they shouldn't be broached in an obligating manner. The demeanor you display in this question should be matter-of fact or just-out-of-curiosity (*unassuming*).

Choice between two positives:
This type of query is only appropriate when a prospect is interested. It is used in an assumptive close. It is obligating in nature and would seem presumptuous if used too soon, or at all.

A choice question is always a choice between two positive alternatives, something or something, not between something and nothing.

Examples
"Would you prefer the black or is gray more to your liking?"
"Do you want delivery on Thursday or would Friday be more convenient?"

Closing Questions
Closing questions presume genuine interest. Until you see or sense this kind of interest, it is important that words, tone, voice inflection, and timing are not too assumptive. Again, the difference between being assumptive and appearing presumptuous, that is, high pressure, is your sensitivity to the real interest of the prospect.

How do you tell when to use a closing question?
This is the purpose of trial close questions combined with proper listening?

Question: What do you do when the trial questions indicate strong interest?

Answer: Do not act at all surprised or in anyway break stride in action, word, tone, or inflection. It is now time to seamlessly transition into closing questions.

Examples:
　　"How does it sound so far?"
　　"What do you like best about it?"

These *obligating* questions should result in interested objections or an opportunity to go right into a standard or direct close.
No response?
How do you respond when you ask a question and there is no response?
(Pensive pause): "Anyway…just a thought."

Remember: You do not actually sell anyone. The better your aptitude and personal sales expertise and proficiency, the better you help prospects buy for themselves.

Listening
Don't ask if you don't intend to listen. When you listen, seem like you are actually listening.

Remember: We love to buy *as much* as we hate to be sold.

> **"To seduce almost anyone, ask for and listen to his opinion"**
> **—Malcolm Forbes**

Questions, used properly, are the best way to accomplish this. Listening without any change in facial expression and body language and without audible sighs is the best way to acquire useful information and set precedence for further questions. By doing this, you will also prevent over-selling.

Aren't good listening skills also just good manners?
The same letters in the word "listen" are in the word "silent."

> "The best way to listen is to stop talking"
> —Red Auerbach

Summary: If you do not know, shouldn't you ask? If prospects do not know, shouldn't you ask them? If you really want to know, shouldn't you actively listen?

Personal Review: Why would *you* buy from you? *Would* you buy from you? Would you *buy* from you? Would you buy from *you* based on the questions you ask and the active listening skills you employ?
If someone else asked the questions, would you buy from him?

Notes: _____

_____
_____
_____
_____
_____
_____
_____
_____
_____
_____

"This makes sense—this works—I can totally do this!"
—Anyone

CHAPTER SEVEN
Forget the Beef. Where's the Sizzle?

Compelling, intriguing, and inspiring presentations (demos) are typically considered the nucleus of the sales process. Although these are an important part of the sales continuum, they constitute only one of the seven building blocks that make up every successful sale.

Finding the hot buttons without adequate pre-approach information is a low-percentage shot. Great pre-approach information enables more directed and intelligent questions to be asked both to gather intelligence and to make compelling points. Most of this can be learned or validated during the qualifying, questioning, and probing step.

As cited in Chapter Four, every step within every phase of the sale is important. Every part is crucial.

Without contact with, or approach to, the prospect, there can be no presentation. Without establishing rapport, that is, creating an emotional connection, there can be no dialogue, trust, interest or semblance of a relationship. Without these vital elements, there would little chance of creating interest, desire or action. As mentioned, some steps of the sale are pre-existing and need not be duplicated.

All the same, *every* part is essential to continuing effectiveness if your immediate goal of that step or phase fits with your ultimate objective.

Most of all, the final result is to establish enduring, satisfied customers who refer and recommend others to you on a regular basis.

The presentation is important for the following reasons:
- Product or service features and benefits are typically expressed in this step.
- Probing questions are asked to gather information.

Trial close questions are used at the first sign of interest shown in the presentation.

> **"If a picture is worth a thousand words, I say a *story* is worth a thousand pictures."**
> **—Me**

What makes a compelling presentation...*compelling*?
You can paint an exquisite picture with the words you choose provided that is your goal. So chose each word you employ with great care.

Evoking the prospect's imagination can be a potent arrow in your sales quiver. To wordsmith is considered both an art and a challenge —well worth the investment of time and brain power.

Simply put...use interesting stories with compelling questions. Direct them toward a single salient point in a minimum time frame.

The value of brevity in a presentation cannot be overstated. Lincoln's "Gettysburg Address" was around one hundred ninety words. The Sermon on the Mount—Jesus' longest recorded speech in the Bible—was less than three thousand words. (150 words per minute—do the math—20 minutes)

> **"Twenty minutes is more than enough time to say the biggest, most important thing in the world."**
> **—President Ronald Reagan**

When you project passion and energy, you communicate. But you must be careful that your words do not get in the way of your meaning.

Prospects typically buy for only one good reason, not a collection of two or three. That single reason is usually exposed or discovered by asking questions in the presentation step.

Identifying W.I.I.F.M. (what's in it for me?) is a vital task during this part of the sale. The best way to accomplish this is through careful observation and, of course, the most appropriate questions.

Features and benefits convey justifications for prospects to become interested in buying. Features refer to what is offered and benefits reveal how features help the prospect solve a problem, save a business, reach a goal, etc.

There is a school of thought that says prospects only buy what they perceive they must buy or what they most want to buy. It follows that they must buy what they want to buy.

W.I.I.F.M. is the real reason people want to buy. Finding that reason as efficiently as possible is the essence of service and a cornerstone of sales.

It is implicit for a company to determine their prospect's unique value statement (UVS). The UVS differentiates what you provide from the perception of what the competition may be offering.

A bargain exists when a prospect believes that the value of what he wants is greater than the investment. The UVS is the bargain when the seller is meeting it.

A stylish presentation
So use a little "poetry." Planned pauses and vocal inflection variations are important considerations. The use of alliterations and rapid lists can go far to maintain interest and provide entertainment.

It's not hard to do, if you pre-plan. Now, on a blank sheet of paper draw a vertical line down the center. Take the left side of the paper and write the name of your idea, product, or service.

Then jot down the most emotional benefits on the right side.

Write every synonym variation you can think of that goes with each word in each column. Use a Thesaurus.

Now mix and match the words you like left to right until you come up with a clever, evocative, catchy, yet clear "handle" for your product.

Try this new branding handle on a variety of people and log all their positive and negative comments.

Examples
"Making salespeople rich and famous"
"Prose for the Prosperous Pros"

Lower your voice, increase your volume
There were a number of instances where a top producer for The Southwestern Company would have an inexplicable spike in sales lasting only a couple of days. It turned out this phenomenon happened concurrently with the onset of laryngitis. Having lost his voice this salesperson was forced to whisper on that particular day!

> **"Words that soak in your ears are whispered…not yelled."**
> **—Cowboy Saying**

Seeing yourself as others see you
Voice recording and video taping presentations allow you to witness what others experience. This practice is an essential part of the educational process. It is an unbelievable eye, ear and mind opener.

Clear, concise, focused, purposeful, and brief
As important as brevity, every presentation must be clear and concise. There can be no room for misunderstanding. Whereas a concise message is an imperative, it plays a distant second to brevity, confidence and enthusiasm in determining a presentation's effectiveness.

Saying many things usually communicates nothing. What makes you so different people should do business with you. Give one reason why.

Beware of esoteric terminology. Speak the prospect's language, not your own. Using obscure jargon may be confusing to a senior level decision maker. It is not just talking over-the-head; it is missing the heart!

The proper use of reference names whenever available before, during, and after the presentation add credibility as well as create and retain interest leading into the close.

Understatement
If there is a feature or a benefit that is too good to be true, it is wise to understate that fact. Even though understatement is not literally the truth, it is not immoral, illegal or fattening, either.

Understating a positive is in no way considered unethical. It is often used to evoke a stronger emotional response from a prospect than if you had stated the obvious.

Examples:
"There is some traffic in Atlanta, right?"
"She is not bad looking, is she?"
"It's chilly, isn't it?" (23 degrees w/ 15 MPH winds)

Exaggeration
Conversely, exaggeration or hyperbole is an onerous type of overselling. A form of misrepresentation because it doesn't tell the truth, it is a sure way to lose credibility.

> "The exact truth *should* be told. They will believe the good, if we candidly tell them the bad also."
> —Thomas Jefferson

Complicity
This is the term used when you allow or lead someone to believe something that is not entirely true. You can do this more by what you don't say or don't do.

Sooner or later this will catch up with you and do irreparable damage to your reputation.

We have all heard the words, "Buyer beware" and "The customer is always right."

As a professional with the customers' best interest at heart and as a top producer with your ultimate objective in mind, your responsibility is to make sure *all your customers are always right.*

The seven deadly sins
Some years ago George Carlin did a comedic routine about the seven words not allowed on daytime television or radio. You can probably guess what they are.

By the same token, there are certain words you should avoid in effective sales presentations. Each word can, and will, trigger negative connotations and create unnecessary hurdles that can prove counterproductive.

If you use these words they will surely work against what you are trying to achieve on behalf of the prospect.

Typical unmentionable words are *buy, sell, price, cost, decide, close,* and *but.*

The positive alternatives are *trying, move forward, became happily involved, lean toward, invest, on track, take care of, use, came to a conclusion,* and *own.*

The word "but" is particularly disagreeable and overused... especially during the close or while handling objections. It tears down empathy and annihilates mutual understanding. When you employ this egregious three-letter word you are, for all practical and reasonable purposes, asking someone to negate all ideas preceding the b-word.

Never a discouraging word
Here is an over-the-top example of too-much-of-a-good-thing.
You may be able to help people *stay on track* to *try* things. They may *lean toward* to help them to *become happily involved* so they *feel comfortable moving forward* thus *allowing them* to *easily invest* in the *value* you present. Nevertheless prospects will easily *take care of it* (payment) and *come to a conclusion* (decide) in order to *enjoy ownership*.

> **"The words we don't use are oft more powerful than the words we employ."**
> **—Anonymous**

No sizzle without meat, no sales without sizzle
Nourishment rich in protein, niacin, riboflavin, thiamine, iron, and phosphorus can lack emotional appeal.

So, *dead cows don't sell*.
Nevertheless, a sizzling piece of choice beef, perfectly prepared and served in an attractive ambiance, sells all day at premium prices. A nice cut of prime beef with the flavor, aroma, texture, and, most of all, the sizzle defines a steak's appeal.

Close your eyes and think about that sizzling steak. You can almost smell it. The emotional and even the physical effects are almost palpable— even to a vegetarian. (Bad prospect for steak!)

Sizzle does more than define the steak. It *sells* the steak—and it does so very efficiently. Am I right or am I wrong?

Your presentation is the sizzle if it incorporates in its story the information gleaned from the pre-approach as well as "qualifying" steps of the sale.

How much is too much? How much is enough?
How long should the presentation be? Depending on the industry you are selling to, an effective demo will generally run anywhere between twenty seconds and twenty minutes.

Edward Everett
Do you know the name Edward Everett? During the mid nineteenth century Everett was the president of Harvard University, Congressman, as well as Senator, and Governor of Massachusetts. He was considered the nation's greatest orator of his time. He was invited to give the main speech at the dedication of the Soldiers' National Cemetery at Gettysburg, Pennsylvania on September 23, 1863.
He told the organizing committee that he would be unable to prepare an appropriate speech in such a short period of time, and requested that the date be postponed. The committee agreed, and the dedication was postponed until November 19.

Almost as an afterthought, David Wills, the president of the committee, asked President Abraham Lincoln to make a "few appropriate remarks."

Everett spoke for two hours. Lincoln's two-minute follow-up speech is one of the most famous speeches in the history of the United States.

The ensuing *informal* comments (speech) are a tribute to what purpose and succinctness of words and delivery can do to the effectiveness of that message. There is much to be said about the impact of these 290 words of rallying the troops behind those "honored dead"

The Gettysburg Address

Four score and seven years ago our fathers brought forth on this continent, a new nation, conceived in liberty, and dedicated to the proposition that all men are created equal.

Now we are engaged in a great civil war, testing whether that nation or any nation so conceived and so dedicated, can long endure. We are met on a great battle-field of that war. We have come to dedicate a portion of that field, as a final resting place for those who here gave their lives that that nation might live. It is altogether fitting and proper that we should do this.

But, in a larger sense, we can not dedicate — we can not consecrate — we can not hallow — this ground. The brave men, living and dead, who struggled here, have consecrated it, far above our poor power to add or detract. The world will little note, nor long remember what we say here, but it can never forget what they did here. It is for us the living, rather, to be dedicated here to the unfinished work which they who fought here have thus far so nobly advanced. It is rather for us to be here dedicated to the great task remaining before us — that from these honored dead we take increased devotion to that cause for which they gave the last full measure of devotion — that we here highly resolve that these dead shall not have died in vain — that this nation, under God, shall have a new birth of freedom — and that government of the people, by the people, for the people, shall not perish from the earth. —**Abraham Lincoln**

Everett wrote a note to Lincoln the next day telling him of his appreciation for the President's brief, but moving, speech: "I would be glad, if I could flatter myself that I came as near the central idea of the occasion in two hours, as you did in two minutes"

"I should be glad, if I could flatter myself that I came as near the central idea of the occasion in two hours, as you did in two minutes."
— Edward Everett

"It is usually and paradoxically true that the more important the message, the less time required saying it."
—Peggy Noonan

How long should a presentation be?
Maybe a more relevant question would be "when should the presentation end (subtle but very important distinction)?"

The answer is surprisingly simple; yet it has always proven one of the greatest challenges in the world of sales.

My best advice is to cease presenting at the first positive change in the prospect's body language or facial expression.

The initial sign of interest should be gently punctuated with an unobtrusive *trial close question.* This type of question is a thermometer to determine if more assumptive closing questions are appropriate and timely.

When all evidence is continuing to move forward at a comfortable pace, do not hesitate as you proceed seamlessly and directly into the close. Doing anything less would represent a gross disservice and project the wrong counter signals. How can someone else believe you if you don't show that you believe you?

Again, please be mindful—the most proficient sales people help prospective customers make the best decisions in the least amount of time.

They go beyond just communicating ideas and motivating people to act upon those ideas. They make the proposal the buyers *own idea* and help the prospects motivate themselves to move on it as soon as possible.

"If you talk a *lot*, people will think you are smart—unless…you keep on talking!" —Anonymous

> **"There is a time to say nothing, and a time to say something, but there is never a time to say everything"— Anonymous**

It's not about *you*; it's about the prospect's needs. Top producers do not allow their verbosity to interfere, no matter how hard it was or long it took to memorize their presentation.

Think about it…what else are you there for?

Summary: Features tell while benefits sell. Presenting benefits with passion mitigates doubt and fear in the prospect's mind. Emotional fervor suggests that you are sold on not only what you're selling but on the belief that your prospect will buy.

Personal Review: Why would *you* buy from you? *Would* you buy from you? Would you *buy* from you? Would you buy from *you* if the presentation didn't engage you and connect with you emotionally?

Notes: _____

_____
_____
_____
_____
_____
_____
_____
_____
_____

> *"This makes sense—this works—I can totally do this!"* —Anyone

CHAPTER EIGHT
What is the Unpardonable Sin?

As the story goes, there was a Catholic girl who fell madly in love with a Methodist boy. Her parents adamantly refused to allow the union. They would not give their blessing due to the difference in religion.

The girl, a proactive aggressive sort, announced she would just have to convert her unsuspecting young beau to Catholicism as to solve the impasse.

She immediately and enthusiastically went to work at the task.

Things seemed to be proceeding quite well until one day the young girl came home crying her eyes out. "The weddings off!" she wailed between inconsolable sobs.

"Why?" her parents inquired. "You seemed to be doing such a good job convincing him of the merits of Catholicism."

"Well, that's the point!" she exclaimed. "I've *over-sold* him and now he wants to be a priest!"

Over-selling is the *unpardonable sin* among novices and seasoned sales pros alike. You work incredibly hard to master your products, presentations, closes, and handling objections. You fall in love with your ideas, products, services, company, hard work, and also the sound of your voice.

Sometimes you don't get positive feedback so you crave the validation of encouraging, amiable comments and reactions demonstrated by the interested prospect. You are so intoxicated with adulation you precede to sabotage

You become a victim of *your* desire to be appreciated.

You fail to practice what you know and what you've learned, which is that *first sign* of interest is the biggest and the best. The "initial interest" is easily twice as good as the second wave and three times that of the third. Again, continuing to present when the first wave occurs is counter to the cause.

Over-selling also projects the wrong signal to the prospective buyer. It demonstrates a lack of confidence and belief on your part.

> **"No sinner was ever saved…after the first twenty minutes of the sermon" –Mark Twain**

An interested prospect becomes confused when they are motivated while you, by your actions, deny validation by not trial closing or closing!

Typically, over-selling has three symptoms:
- No interest evident or perceived on the part of the prospect
- Overlooking or misreading closing opportunities
- Fear of rejection and failure

By far the most common of these is *fear of rejection and failure*. We should be reminded it's "not about us". Selling is helping prospects buy over and over again while encouraging their immediate sphere of influence to do likewise.

You don't ask—they can't tell
If you don't ask, they can't say "no." They also can't show you how to help them buy. And you make it harder and harder for them to say "yes." That is why it is so important to remind yourself that selling is all about helping the prospect. It is *not* about you.

A top salesperson's job is to find a need and fill it in the least amount of time. No more, no less. Every clever phrase, interesting question, and compelling story beyond that watershed or bellwether moment diminishes the chances of helping the prospect buy.

Question:
"Are you with me so far?" "Yes" (said with appropriate tone, facial expression, and body language)
"Any questions so far?" "No"
"How does it sound so far?" "Great!"
"All we need is a couple of pieces of paper—can we get started?" "OK!"

Note: It would be hypocritical for me to say more about this subject—so this will be the shortest chapter. Doing otherwise would be *overselling*.

Summary: Oversell? Don't.

Personal Review: Would *you* buy from you? Why w*ould* you buy from you? Why would you *buy* from you? Would you buy from *you*? Isn't overselling like taking a horse to water and *not* letting it drink?

Notes: _____

_____
_____
_____
_____
_____
_____
_____
_____
_____

"This makes sense—this works—I can totally do this!" —Anyone

CHAPTER NINE

Call Reluctance, Fear of Rejection and failure, and Other Emotional Hurdles

Thinking and acting outside the box is both one of the most challenging and rewarding of human activities. Most of us denounce the thought of playing games to fool our emotions. Nonetheless, we subconsciously allow ourselves this indulgence to maintain our self-image equilibrium don't we? Be honest with yourself.

Fears are some of the strongest motivations we experience daily. Pain, dying, the unknown, appearing dumb, sounding stupid, being misunderstood, having feelings hurt: these are just a few of the things people fear.

Fear of failure, public speaking, and rejection can be attributed to a strong desire to preserve fragile egos. We often fear what others might think of us. These emotional trepidations are often a major cause of procrastination. Some of the putting-off the task manifestations include obsessively straightening the papers on a desk, sleeping in or drinking an extra cup of coffee. Avoiding exposure to something you fear to face, either consciously or subconsciously, is the goal. It is a goal not worth reaching. Procrastination is the greatest deterrent of success.

Fear of success is more common than you might think…especially if you view yourself as lucky or not deserving of that success.

Fear of rejection is such a noxious and physically incapacitating feeling you will do anything or believe any lame rationale to avoid situations in which you could potentially be turned down.

It is normal human behavior to buy into plausible excuses to justify errant behavior. But once you realize why you are fooling yourself you can begin to take charge of the mental games you play.

"Our doubts and fears are traitors making us lose the good we might oft obtain by causing us *not* to try."
—Anonymous

"I believe that anyone can conquer fear by doing the things he fears to do, provided he keeps doing them until he gets a record of successful experiences behind him."
—Eleanor Roosevelt

What can you do to overcome negatives caused by fear?

Shout Out Loud!
The most proven antidote to losing the self-speak battle between your ears is to proactively engage in repetitious **out-loud** positive affirmations. Talk to yourself in the shower or in the car until you emotionally *feel* what you are saying.

No substitute for action
After out-loud affirmations, the best and only remedy for fear is *action*. It may sound simplistic; nevertheless in practice it works every time all the time! The only way to overcome fear is to form the habit of doing the very things you fear.

> **"Do the things you fear and the death of fear is certain."**
> **—Emerson**

Think of all the *firsts* in your life. Reflect on the first time you rode a bike, jumped into deep water, or spoke in front of a group. It is obvious this principle applies throughout life.

Doing the thing you fear is not the *best* way to build confidence; it is the *only* way to develop true confidence! This applies even more in an activity as proactive as personal sales calls.

Some may even think personal sales as a career is masochistic. I contend that not confronting the fear of rejection is more than masochistic it is almost sadistic!

> **"One of the cruelest of vicious cycles is for someone to waste their life waiting for courage to do the things that, in fact, would give them the courage they need."**
> **—Anonymous**

Directly, the converse reinforces the point. There are plenty of people who harbor fears of swimming, dark rooms, speaking before groups or the unknown simply because they hesitated to the point of debilitation earlier in life when they experienced the emotion. The first time may seem the toughest, yet each time you avoid the challenge it gets harder.

Habits
We are slaves to all our habits. It typically takes twenty-one days to form any of the habits of which we want to be enslaved. This is true of either good or bad habits. Isn't defining which you prefer the better game to play?

> **"The secret of success for every person who has been successful lies in the fact that he or she has formed the habit of doing things failures don't like to do."** — Albert Gray, *The Common Denominator of Success*

Doesn't it make sense to choose good habits over bad?

Summary: Have you ever tried to change one of your own habits?

Personal Review: Keep in mind that you have no vested interest. You do not have to buy from you. Why would *you* buy from you? *Would* you buy from you? Would you *buy* from you? Would you buy from *you*...if you didn't show up on time and failed to call? Whose time is more important...Yours, or your prospects? Ask the prospect whose time is more important.

Notes:

"This makes sense—this works—I can totally do this!"
—Anyone

CHAPTER TEN
Third Parties Make the World Go Round

One (first party) would come considerably closer to persuading another (second party) by properly using "they or them" in the third party. Put more simply. The first gets somewhere with the second when the first utilized the third. Does that make sense?

The effective use third party references or referrals are fundamental to successful selling. *Third party* is used in obtaining attention, creating curiosity, and engendering credibility. It can be used in almost any part of the cycle of the sale if it is used appropriately

Improper utilization of this tool can spell disaster in that it may be viewed as blatant *name dropping* thus destroying the rapport' and trust previously established. It is most effective when mentioned with no presumption as a *matter of fact* only for your information type attitude.

If the prospect is not a long time trusted friend with whom you have a strong relationship, any suggestions you make first party may be viewed with some degree of suspicion. This natural skepticism is greatly mitigated by the appropriate use of a third party illustration. This is especially true during initial contact, presenting features and benefits, as well as in closing the sale

How the third-party strategy is best utilized?

Using third party in the initial contact:
"Bill, I don't think we've met—Jane Smith told me you were one of the good guys—anyway (interrupting yourself), I promised I would give you a call. Here's why…"

Go blind creating curiosity without making an obvious *quid pro quo*.
"Joe, a couple of people whom you know (are friends with, do business with) told me some very flattering things about you and said we needed to talk. I'll tell you later who they are but they said I had an idea that would be of benefit to you and visa-versa. It's 3 PM on Tuesday afternoon. I'm giving you my cell phone so we can avoid telephone tag. It's 555-5555. It would be great if you had a chance to reach me before 5"

When using this type of blind "third party" approach it is best to assume an attitude of nonchalance. i. e. tone down the enthusiasm. The more powerful the words you use, the less emphasis you need put behind them. As in every case, it's not as much what you say as it is how you say it.

Using third party in the presentation:
"John, here is what Bill Anderson and the XYZ company liked best about this feature…"

"You might know some of the other companies who have moved forward on this…"

Using third party in Closing:
"Jane Jones took advantage of this for three reasons:
- increased savings
- improved earnings
- a competitive advantage

Just out of curiosity, what appeals to you most?"

Reply: "I agree with everything!"

You: "This *would* give you an increased competitive advantage, wouldn't it?" (Tie-down question)
Reply: "Yes, it would"

You: "All we need are a couple of pieces of paper to get started. (Do not pause) Can I get those from you today?" (Assumptive paperwork close)

When using third party illustrations, always assume the *second* party will invariably check with the *third* party and assume anything that can be misunderstood will be misunderstood. Always ask for and receive clear, unambiguous consent from the third party and always explain exactly how and when you will use their name. Explain it twice (two variations) to make sure everything is clear.

Third party adds credibility, creates rapport', and engenders trust if used properly and correctly. It has the opposite effect if not properly executed. Take a chance…third-party saves time and makes it easy to buy.

Summary: Someone very close to you told me if I used their name you would like me and trust me? Or maybe they were just saying if I didn't mention them you wouldn't even give me the time of day?

Personal Review: Would *you* buy from you? *Would* you buy from you? Why would you *buy* from you? Would you buy from *you* if you didn't properly use third party every chance you could?

Notes:
_____
_____
_____
_____
_____
_____
_____
_____
_____
_____

"This makes sense—this works—I can totally do this!"—Anyone

CHAPTER ELEVEN
Not Listening, Not Hearing

Volumes have been written on the art of listening. Frankly, there is not much point in asking questions unless you carefully pay attention to the answers, is there? Isn't that the point of asking? How else do you learn what is on the prospect's mind and in his heart?

The function of actively listening has three important benefits:
- It shows the prospective customer you are indeed interested in him
- The information gathered tells you how to best serve the prospect
- People love to talk, it puts them at ease and creates rapport

Learning begins with understanding, which begins with better listening skills. It almost goes without saying that understanding the needs of the prospect is essential to helping them buy.

> **"If I were to summarize in one sentence the single most important principle in the field of interpersonal relationships, listening is the key."** —Stephen Covey

Everyone likes a good listener, especially your prospects. All this is in keeping with the first premise of this book: people love to buy as much as they hate to be sold.

The prospects can do a pretty good job of selling themselves if you keep quiet and allow them to talk about their needs and motives.

The most effective salesperson learns from actively listening. Active listening is most effective when there are minimal distractions or interruptions.

In personal sales, it is the professional who finds the most optimum setting possible. Even the smallest detail must be taken into account.

For example, if the sales venue is a restaurant, select one most conducive to talking and listening. Seat yourself facing the door to decrease possible distractions for your prospect. It may sound elementary but do try to find a relatively quiet restaurant.

Active listening mandates that every action, facial expression and mannerism display the same understanding and respect you value.

Most of us have had the experience in a social situation of talking to someone who was panning the crowd with their eyes. If you felt a bit offended with his or her lack of attention, how must your prospective customer feel when you do likewise?

Another huge mistake is to show lack of concern for the prospect's feelings. Psychologically speaking, one cannot imply that another individual does not feel the way he feels. He feels that way and you can only surmise why and simply inquire without showing the slightest prejudice.

Simply asking permission to take a few notes, along with rudimentary verbal validation, is more than just flattering. It is an excellent way to demonstrate a true regard for the prospect as a fellow human being. It sets precedence.

As one gets closer to a decision, a prospect becomes increasing susceptible to anything perceived as insensitivity or lack of empathy on the part of the influencer.

People are funny. We can't help ourselves. We love a great listener, someone who validates our feelings and our thinking while stroking our fragile egos.

Summary: Are you listening? Are you actually hearing?

Personal Review: Would *you* buy from you? *Would* you buy from you? Would you *buy* from you? Would you buy from *you* if you didn't show you cared enough to actively listen?

Notes:

"This makes sense—this works—I can totally do this!"
—Anyone

CHAPTER TWELVE
Drivers Drive, Thinkers Think, and Buyers Buy

Not all buyers act alike in a sales situation. Different personalities respond well, differently. This is especially true at the beginning and at the close in the decision process.

Three of the most prevalent personality types, traits or styles are:
- The *aggressive* prospect, called a driver
- The *analytical* decision maker, called the thinker
- The *followers*, prospective buyers referred to as socially popular

Most buyers share part of all three buying personality traits. Nevertheless, everyone displays a single dominant propensity.

Drivers distinguish themselves early in the set-up by showing some signs of impatience. It is not uncommon for them to interrupt you during the set-up saying, "What do you want?" or "How can I help you?" They know they cannot allow themselves to show interest. They view it as a sign of vulnerability or weakness. Still, drivers may be excellent prospects.

Drivers are sometimes insecure about tipping their hand to anyone they view as trying to sell them. This is their defense mechanism. This is their game and it requires the sales professional to temporarily play along until the driver begins to understand what is in his enlightened self-interest. Not only is it a game; it is the driver's way of testing how much you are sold on your own services.

Selling is not intellectual combat with a winner and a loser. Ideally, it is purely win-win by finding a need and filling it. However, there are those that treat the sales experience as an adversarial game. Being aware and understanding this dynamic helps you deal with drivers.

What is the most effective way to deal with someone acting this way? Let them drive. This calls for the most succinct elevator speech and a strong demonstration of active listening skills. Enjoy the ride while they drive. Demonstrate your willingness to allow them to dominate until they acquiesce and believe you have their best interest at heart.

Analytical (thinker) prospects see decision making more as a process than an event. This process typically takes more time than other buying personality types. Rapport is less difficult than with drivers. The presentation is typically, but not always, longer with the analytical than other prospect types. They are more methodical in process. Understanding this is vital. You are in the driver's seat; the analytical prospect is riding.

Any attempt to move the thinker forward before he believes he has had the time to analyze may create grave consequences.

Overly aggressive closing, also known as "high pressure", can destroy rapport, credibility, and any potential relationship leading to a positive buying decision. The antidote is to give the analytical time needed to process and appreciate the information. Obtain a commitment to their decision process and time frame and then follow-up.

The follower, or socially popular, type is influenced by others. Followers do not necessarily buy because it is the popular thing to do. They are not likely to even start listening with a mind toward making decisions unless they are convinced that everyone else is doing it.

Moreover, the positive feelings they experience during the sales process must be validated by colleagues. Getting all the decision influencers together for a first or second presentation is essential.

The term "herd mentality" comes immediately to mind in dealing with followers, who are the most prevalent of buying personality types. Few people can buy in a vacuum. That's why God created shopping malls!

Yet it is understandable why so many people deny that they are followers rather than independent minded leaders. No one wants to believe they are influenced by what others do. It does not fit our preferred self-image.

Most of us prefer to see ourselves as much more of an analytical, independent thinking and assertive buyer than is actually the case.

In light of this information the best way for effective sales producers to help most prospects decide becomes obvious. Use the names of the influencers in the approach, set-up, presentation, and close.

Do your best to be subtle. The art of appearing matter-of-fact or "just-for-your-information" is essential in the use of influencers' names.

No one likes a blatant name dropper. Names are powerful sales tools to be used with some discretion; there is always a point of diminishing returns. Too much of a good thing…you know the rest.

In the set-up or rapport building phase pay close attention to pacing, Mirror your actions, tone, inflection, speech patterns, and body language to that of the prospect.

It is incumbent upon you to find common ground and determine the type of prospect with which you are dealing. You can then adjust your unique style to theirs to engage them, build interest and, so to speak, get on his side of the desk. The relationship will either build or deteriorate. Like all other human relations and all nature it is dynamic.

Signals during the set-up or rapport
As you enter the prospect's office you are presented with a plethora of less than subtle hints about the type of prevailing personality type you are encountering. This is also your clue to the rapport-building subject matter you may verbally note.
Let's say the prospect has three sailfish on the wall or sixteen framed pictures of children and grandchildren. If you do not comment on these clues, what are you not thinking?
By coupling these indicators with what you learned previously about the prospect from the referrer and other sources, you can get a pretty good idea with whom you are trying to communicate.

Adapt, adjust, and know how your personality type meshes with theirs.

If you can only relate to personalities the same as yours, you will have a limited target market.

Summary: There is no one-size-fits-all. What kind of buyer and what kind of salesperson are you?

Personal Review: Would *you* buy from you? *Would* you buy from you? Would you *buy* from you? Would you buy from *you* if you were not cognitive of—or adjusting to—perceived differences in buyer personalities? Would you meet you half way? The responsibility rests with you— the seller.

Notes:

"This makes sense—this works—I can totally do this!"
—Anyone

CHAPTER THIRTEEN
Disparities Between What's Sold and What's Delivered

The ultimate sales objective is to have a long-term, low-maintenance customer volunteering as a great reference.

The company or organization believes it know what it offers. The salesperson believes he understands what the company can deliver. The prospect/customer believes he understands that which the salesperson is offering relative to his needs.

What can possibly be wrong with this picture? Are we dealing with three possibly different and incongruent perceptions?

Any disparities between what is expected and the perception of what is delivered will eventually rear its ugly head at the most detrimental time.

Salespeople share responsibility with the company but the onus falls on the sales professional to insure the compatibility between perceptions. The salesperson's job and reputation mandate this. That's why the personal sales pro is the go-between with the greatest opportunity to see what's happening and "make it right."

The sales professional stands to lose the most in the long run if there is any disparity between what is said, what is understood and what is delivered. The salesperson did not cause—but rather allowed—the lose-lose corollary.

The problems caused by this disparity scenario can carry out virtually irreversible damage to the client relationship.

The only solution is prevention. The best prevention is facing reality. Objectivity requires winning the battle between what you want to believe and what others will believe in the long term.

Please notice I sidestepped the word "truth" because perception is for all practical purposes…reality. Truth is relative more to what one wants to believe than to what actually is.

In personal sales you must deal with every individual prospect's perception. If the prospect or the customer feels unhappy, you can kiss that long-term relationship good-bye along with the good reference.

As usual, the solution is both simple and logical. After the dust has settled for a few weeks or months, ask the client exactly why he bought and what he now thinks about the product/service. After getting the candid customer feedback, do likewise with the management responsible for providing product/service.

Analyze both pieces of information. If they do not reasonably equate, if there is little or no cooperation from your company, if you cannot make adjustments or tweaks to the presentation or sales strategy to address the issue, you have a problem detrimental to acquiring future business.

The company is living on income derived solely on new business created in spite of the disparity between expectations and reality.

If the company chooses to ignore the problem, thinking it will go away on its own accord, you face an insurmountable obstacle.

The suggestion I am about to make is based on personal experience. Get out as fast as you can. Try to cash in your options and wash your hands. Things will only get worse!

Always keep firmly in mind that your ultimate objective is to cultivate loyal, satisfied customers who are constant source of good references.

With that in the front of your conscience mind you must face the hard, cold reality that a company cannot long survive when it does not take care of existing customers.

> "If you think you can enrich yourself by deluding others, you can only end up deluding yourself." —Earl Nightingale

If you lead a sales organization—you will naturally be held to a higher standard by your followers. For their sake you will be well served to remind yourself that leading by example is not the best way, it's the only way to lead.

> "You cannot teach what you do not know. You cannot lead where you will not go."
> —William 'Brave Heart' Wallace

Summary: Be accountable to be responsible.

Personal Review: Would *you* buy from you? *Would* you buy from you? Why would you *buy* from you? Would you buy from *you* if you learned there was irrevocable disparity between what was promised and what was delivered?

Notes:

"This makes sense—this works—I can totally do this! —Anyone

CHAPTER FOURTEEN
Prospects, References, Referrals

Prospects versus *suspects*
According to demographics and available information, a prospect is someone with expressed or implied needs, wants, or interest in your product/service, along with the capacity to pay. This is preferably an individual or firm that has been referred to you by an existing loyal, satisfied client. You have done your homework. You have a goal and a plan.

How does a prospect differ from a suspect?
You have no pre-approach information on a suspect telling you there is likelihood for attention and interest. Also, you have no relationship to anyone with any information or influence over a suspect.

Best prospects
What factors make up the prospects most likely to want to become satisfied with your products/services?

A person or organization much like your existing best clients makes the best prospects. These good prospects are accessible, approachable and available and have the means to invest in your products or services.

You gather information that helps you approach and gain the attention of this prospect.

How do you find the best prospects?
Go to your best customers and ask for referrals. It is not at all uncommon for even the best of clients not to realize you want and need referrals. Getting referrals and references tells you how satisfied your existing customers are.

The way to request referrals determines quality and quantity. If you we ask or offer suggestions on how you can better serve the existing customers you may earn the right to ask for references. Likewise, you can offer additional enhancements or services to encourage them to help with references.

Anticipate objections before they become an issue. Do this by empathizing with the customer and by putting yourself in their shoes.

Think, "Why would I hesitate giving a referral to me?"

Determining the answer to this question gives you the words needed to defuse fears and put the client at ease.

Example:
"Sue, you have been a great customer for many years. We are looking to expand our services in the City? Do you mind if I use your name as a reference from time to time? I do not want to help your direct competition. Who are some folks you relate to who are not direct competitors and might like to know about my services, "even if only for future reference"?

Who do you know in Farmers Branch? How about Denton? Are you friends with anyone in Cleburne? Is their operation a lot like yours? Are they about the same size, type, etc? Who is the likely decision maker?

Who would you talk to over there if you were calling on them?

If I use it appropriately; may I use your name?"

If you have a longstanding positive relationship you may try a less orthodox approach like this:

You (Tongue-in-cheek): "Joe, you must be unhappy with the job we are doing for you."

Prospect: "Why do you say that?"

You: "Well, if we were doing a great job you would refer us to other good companies like yours, wouldn't you?"

If you ask specifics about referred targeted prospects you're you will better your success ratio in your approach.

Example
"I'm thinking about talking to ABC Inc. Are they direct competitors of yours? How well do you know them? If you were me who would you talk to over there? Do you mind if I mention your name if I don't overuse or misuse it?"

It is common courtesy to show appreciation for help. This may include gifts, reduced price services, or the like.

Additionally, it is thoughtful and good business practice to report back good news regarding referrals.

All of this offers further opportunity for relationship-building customer contact. An existing customer's cooperation is an accurate barometer for the ongoing relationship.

Number of prospects
How many prospects do you need on your hot list?
This is in part determined by several factors, the:

- Rate at which the business can grow
- Total number of qualified prospects in your territory
- Proximity of the prospects
- Current number of satisfied customers (references) in your territory
- Average sales cycle
- Average closing ratio
- Support/training/delivery staff
- Sales production goals

Sales production goals have the *greatest* affect on all other factors. Moreover, all the other factors affect sales goals.

It is the classic "Catch-22". You cannot or should not sell that which you cannot support. Conversely you may be unable to support, deliver, manufacture, advertise, market, or staff-up for that which can sell.

Failing to heed this axiom has been the downfall of many great, or potentially great, companies.

The micro-economics of this truism are far-reaching. It can be the primary cause of many other grave political and organizational ailments.

How to get a reference letter of recommendation
The written word is more credible than the spoken word.
How do you get a reference letter? Take a good client to lunch, dinner, coffee or a game and simply ask for it. If the client hesitates for no apparent reason, suggest you write one and let him edit, sign it, and put on his letterhead.

Note: Do not date the copy. The date is not important and it may be distracting to others in the future. Another good idea is to show the good client other reference letters just prior to asking for one.
How do you use a reference letter? Show it early and often, especially if the prospect has a relationship with your client. Read the letter to the prospect if the person agrees.

As in any art you have to think and show some sensitivity to the situation. As in any human interaction you must not assume the other person will do what you wish on his or her own discretion.

The Hot List Formula
How many referrals or prospects do you need on the hot list?
- If the budget, business plan, and scalability allow for eight new accounts in a six-month time frame
- If there are sufficient potential prospects in the salesperson's territory
- If the potential referrals are within a 2 hour trip (1 salesperson; 3 travel days/ week)
- If the business has 5 cooperating, loyal, satisfied customers willing to refer (out of 20 potentials)
- If the average sales cycle is 4 weeks
- If the average closing ratio is 1-out-of-5 qualified referral prospects
- If the support staff can take care of current business and new business with no sacrifice in quality

Here is the well guarded confidential "magic formula":
- Subtract the sales cycle from the total sales campaign goal (6 months -1 month = 5 months.)
- Determine how many calls are required (on average) to contact a referral or a prospect. Make a note of the best times to contact people depending upon the industry.
- Divide the contact goals and call goals by days and best time of day.

Surprise! Surprise! The answer will always be arbitrary because there are so many random variables outside your control.

The secret is to set a series of 21-day activity habits with no variance. If you fall behind, it is unwise to *stack* goals. Stacking goals adds undue pressure and, in turn may cause you to appear desperate. Just trust the law of averages and develop self-discipline, consistency and a sense of urgency one step at a time.

Once you sell one, replace the hot prospect within a week. Never allow the pipeline go dry.
Never make yourself start over.

Summary: The more you use references and recommendations you cultivate the easier it is for your prospects to relate to you, trust you, learn from you and buy from you. Prospects want to do what's best. It's even better when it sounds like it is also what is most popular!

Personal Review: Would *you* buy from you? *Would* you buy from you? Why would you *buy* from you? Would you buy from *you* if you if you were a stranger cold calling on you?

Notes:
_____
_____
_____
_____
_____
_____
_____
_____
_____
_____

"This makes sense—this works—I can totally do this!"—Anyone

CHAPTER FIFTEEN
Reaching Decision Makers

What is the key to knowing who the real decision maker is? Ask the reference and anyone else in a position to give an objective answer. If you ask a person who does not know, he may tell you who *does* know.

This pre-approach information will prove invaluable to saving time for everyone involved in the sales process.

Most often the President and/or CEO make the decisions. The President/CEO is always concerned about wasting time and looking bad. The average decision maker has been tricked into wasting valuable time with inept salespeople lacking the expertise, professionalism, products, or services that help the decision maker buy and look good for doing so.

The gatekeeper
Because the decision maker has been burned in the past he or she relies on a skilled gatekeeper to protect their time. This person is a most important asset to the decision maker. Screening sales people is an integral part of that job, and gatekeepers can be very territorial.

Much has been said regarding pre-approach. Part of that pre-approach is to learn everything you can about the gatekeeper.

Ask the receptionist or another employee the name and correct pronunciation of the executive's administrative assistant. Do not refer to the person as secretary. You must also make sure you know what the decision maker is called. There are few things worse than referring to the top guy as Herman while those who know him call him Trey!

A gatekeeper can be your best friend or your worst enemy if you do not do your homework and treat him or her with due respect.

Example of Phone Approach
Always be smiling when you are on the phone. People *can* tell.
You (smiling): "Is this Sue Johnson? This is (your name). Ed Smith (good reference) and I are working together on a little project he thought Trey would want to hear about. Is Trey in?"

Sue: "Does Trey know you?"

You (smiling): "Oh, no Sue, Ed Smith suggested I meet with Trey; is he around?"

Sue: "What is the name of your company?"

You (smiling): "Sue, Trey would not know me or my company, but he does know Ed. I understand you have been with Trey for over 10 years. Do you set Trey's appointments or will I need to talk directly with him?" (assumptive without being presumptuous)

Sue: "Could you tell me a little bit about what you are doing? He may want you to meet with someone else."

You (smiling) "Sue, this is for CEO's only; that's why Ed Smith thought I should see Trey."

Sue: "Well Trey is on the phone right now."

You (smiling): "Sue, I know it is hard to tell but, do you think he will be a long time or could he be finished any minute? (No pause) I don't mind holding.

Sue: "It's hard to tell."

You (smile) "That's OK, Sue. If you don't mind, if it's not too much trouble and if it's all right with you, why don't I just hold a few minutes? I'm trying to avoid phone tag and I promised Ed I would get in touch with Trey.

Sue: "That's OK with me."

Note:
You would stay with Sue only if she showed no overt signs of anxiety. In this illustration the gatekeeper (Sue) was good-natured and professional. You were focused, considerate and pleasantly persistent.

Here what to do when Trey picks up the phone
Trey: "Hello, may I help you?"

You (smiling): "Trey? This is (your name). Ed Smith (good reference) talked to me about you the other day. You and Ed go way back, don't you?"

Trey: "Yes, Ed and I started our business about the same time. We sometimes golf together."

You (smiling): "Well Trey, Ed told me some very good things about you and your business. Anyway (interrupt yourself to maintain focus), Ed and I are working together on a program he said you should at least hear about 'even if only for future reference'. I promised him I would get with you so that's why I am calling."

Trey: "What is it all about?"

You (smiling) "Ed said you'd ask that. Trey, it is impossible to *explain even in part* over the phone. However, I am in Atlanta on Wednesday or Thursday. Can you pull away from your busy schedule for a few minutes either of those days?"

What if Trey is amenable to meeting and is slammed on those two days?

You (smiling): "That's OK. There is no rush. How does next week or the week after look. I can meet very early or very late if that helps you." (Stop and listen)

Trey: "Could you send some information? I may want to put you with someone else."

You (smiling) "Sure, I could. However, I can explain it faster than you can read it. I can answer your questions if you become interested, and this is *for CEO's only*. (Don't pause) How about sometime next week? I can be very brief."

Trey: "OK, how about this Thursday morning early?"

This part of selling is definitely a game that tests a real pro's resolve. If you are not sold on sales, if you are not sold on yourself and your value propositions, you lose this game by default. Is that your intention?

Your goal is not to employ tricks and gimmicks to persuade people to buy. Professional selling is not a list of secret killer questions and phrases meant to outsmart or outwit the prospect.

Yes, cold calls work, depending on the industry, but they rarely achieve your goals over the long haul.

Your ultimate objective is building a relationship during the sales process that leads to long-term loyal clients and consistent references. You do not sell. You help others buy.

Summary: Reach the right person the right way. Travel is expensive and your time is valuable. There is no room in the budget for wasted time.

Personal Review: Would **you** buy from you? **Would** you buy from you? Would you **buy** from you? Would you buy from **you** if you hadn't spent two minutes to get the pre-approach from third party prior to the approach?

Notes:

"This makes sense—this works—I can totally do this!"
—Anyone

CHAPTER SIXTEEN
The Simple Genius

It may sound contradictory or even paradoxical, but you must be pretty smart to make things *simple*. There is a well-known adage in the personal sales world that states, "Confused prospects don't buy." How could they possibly appreciate what they cannot understand?

They do not necessarily need to know how a watch, a car, or a computer *works* to buy that particular item. The prospect only needs the simplest and most succinct answer to W.I.I.F.M. (What's in it for me?)

An even better well-known saying is K.I.S.S. The first time I heard this I was back in high school. K.I.S.S. stood for "keep it simple stupid." Later, it was considered more politically correct to say "keep it simple salesperson." I got the message even though I had no idea how difficult it was to accomplish this in practice. Simple sells. Complex can't.

> **"Anything that can be misunderstood *will* be misunderstood in the worst possible way!"—Murphy**

A prospect in the presence of any salesperson is certainly out of his/her "comfort zone". Their actions and reactions can range from atypical to bizarre to even dishonest. (Yes, good people lie to salespeople!)

Recall the times you entered a retail clothing store. The sales clerk may have greeted you with the polite inquiry, "May I help you?" Upon being approached you may have experienced uncomfortable emotions. Even though you went into the establishment for good reason you found yourself almost automatically saying, "Oh no, I am just looking."

Again, this alien behavior occurs among honest, confident, intelligent individuals. Why do prospects react this way?

Prospects have an ingrained adversarial relationship with those whom they view as the stereotypical salesperson. Prospects do not give sales people the benefit-of-the-doubt. Initially they treat all sales people alike. It is a simple fact of life.

Because of this dynamic, prospective customers are mentally and emotionally on-guard. Their minds race wildly in an attempt to understand what is being offered without so much as trying to listen to what is being said.

This paradox is especially unfortunate if the sales professional truly has the prospect's best interest at heart with a product or service that solves the prospect's problems.

It is like a veterinarian trying to put a bandage on a wounded dog. There is just an emotional failure to communicate.

This brings the point home. The pre-approach, approach, set-up, presentation—every part of the sale—should keep this phenomenon squarely in mind.

Confused customers do not buy. Neither do intimidated or scared customers. The process of direct selling is very *uncomfortable* for the majority of people because of their prior experiences.

> **"I know you believe you understand what you *think* I said. I am just not sure that what you heard is what I *meant*!"**
> **—Anonymous**

Earlier the importance of the set-up was covered. Without the rapport, trust, and empathy from this early part of the sale the prospect's mind is going in many directions and thinking about everything other than the presentation or value proposition.

When you ask someone for directions on a mobile phone while driving, what is the first thing the other party asks? "Where are you now?"

The questions you use will tell you where your prospect is. This info is necessary to taking the prospect to where he or she needs to go.

Even the best prospects get ahead of your presentation because they believe that they know where you are going. They believe they already know everything you are saying and everything you are about to say. They even believe they know what they are supposed to think about it. It is a human defense mechanism, a method for maintaining their comfort zone.

Thinking is hard work. It is uncomfortable. You are attempting to get prospects to think without making them feel uncomfortable. This is a delicate, yet important balance.

Summary: Simply put; simple sells. Confusion can't!

Personal Review: Would *you* buy from you? Why *would* you buy from you? Why would you *buy* from you? Would you buy from *you* if you were confused and misunderstood the value of the proposition?

Notes:

"This makes sense—this works—I can totally do this!"
—Anyone

CHAPTER SEVENTEEN
Wrench the Heart without Wrinkling the Shirt

The Art of Closing

What is closing?
Is it an art? Is it a science? Can it be both art and science?

Sir Winston Churchill would have put it this way in his distinctive heavy English accent, "How do I explain the close? It is a riddle inside a mystery…wrapped in an enigma!"

Common misconception
There is negative stereotype all too many inside and outside of sales ascribe. It is that closing is *forcing people to do things they don't want to do*. Unfortunately this does precisely describe *bad* closing. This is *de facto* what a great many salespeople do. Unfortunately, sometimes it works.

Why Close the Sale?
Closing is the essence of selling. Selling without closing is just polite conversation and more useful for *making* friends rather than *helping* friends.

And again, if you need a buddy, get a dog. I know that sounds harsh, but your objective is to help people move forward on what best serves their needs, not just meeting for a friendly chat.

Building relationships before, during and after the close plays a valuable role in the sales process. But let's be honest. By *not* closing you are allowing yourself to creatively avoid your responsibility to serve those people with whom you are building a relationship.

All parts of the sale – from gathering referrals to pre-approach, and presentation—are done with closing as the primary goal.

There is a school of thought called ABC, or Always Be Closing. Although a bit simplistic, this is accepted modus operandi. In most cases, taken to heart and poorly implemented. ABC can be too aggressive.

It is a far, far better thing that you always angle for the final result while alertly seeking the first and best opportunity to "trial close".
Overtly closing or closing too soon, too late, or too aggressively can destroy rapport or at least diminish the chances of building the proper relationship to serve the customer.

You should rarely ask an obligating, or closing, question prior to a non-obligating or trial closing, question. Properly reading the answer to the trial close question is vital to moving the process smoothly along. You can always ask a second trial close question for clarification sake.

When to Close

Setting up the close begins in the approach
As you establish rapport or if rapport pre-exists you can or should let the prospect know what you have in mind for the meeting. Subtlety and nonchalance are paramount to accomplish your purpose.

Your intention is to communicate the following ideas in an unobtrusive manner:

"John, my job is to help (<u>business owners, bakers, candlestick makers, etc.</u>) like yours reach your goals. I don't know if I can do that for you in a way that will suit your situation.

"Why don't I ask just you a couple of questions? If I think I have something that will make you more effective, efficient, productive, and profitable, I'll tell you. If not, I'll tell you that, as well. Does that make sense? Are you with me so far?"

Here is another variation on the same theme. This approach to setting up the close early requires a strong relationship and no small amount of confidence where you have presently or previously built up an abundance of goodwill.

Example:
"Jane, I can give you enough information so when we are finished you will be able to say 'yes' or 'no.' If the answer is 'no' that won't hurt my feelings one bit. Does that sound fair?"

Warning: A positive, truly helpful attitude is absolutely essential to achieving the desired result. You are trying to produce accountability without inadvertently causing unseemly "high pressure." This step is both difficult and necessary in helping the prospect realize the goals he or she want to achieve.

When your objectives match the prospect's goals, everyone wins. After all, isn't that everyone's ultimate goal?

> # "You've got to ask for the business!"
> # —Anonymous

Closing during the presentation
It is a worthy and realistic goal to always take advantage of a closing opportunity prior to the end of any sales presentation. The earlier you trial close the better.

Closing within the demo requires sensitivity to buying signs, moods, timing and the between-the-lines meaning of the prospect's responses. All of this is taken in consideration in the context and politics of the moment. Each sales call is singular in nature.

A combination of aggressiveness and sensitivity is the difference between a good and a great close to a good sales call.

Misnomer
I am a believer that the word "close" may be an inappropriate expression for what is really the beginning of an enduring business relationship. This is especially apropos in light of the ultimate goal discussed earlier which is to create a lasting, satisfied customer who volunteers regularly as an excellent reference.

One-call closing
One-call closing is especially appropriate for selling tangible consumer goods and in easily understood less expensive product and service offerings. Nevertheless, it is a goal for every sale.

In the relationship business where most personal selling resides, one-call closing can mean easy come and easy go. Love at first sight relationships often end quickly. The customer may be buying based on a misunderstanding of the terms, the value, or the commitment. Buyers' remorse or competitors' correcting the prospects decision may result.

So when is the best time to close? The answer doesn't change: Close at the *first* hint of interest.

The explanation behind this apparent contradiction may lie with projecting the appropriate message of the ultimate goal. That's because closing to the "next step" is part of building the relationship.

Closing to the next step may be the best close

The next step can be:
- Meeting with the other decision makers and/or decision influencers
- Setting up the decision process to facilitate the final action
- Finding or setting the decision time table

How do you determine the first sign of interest?
Watch, listen, and observe any change in the body language, tone, voice inflection, breathing pattern, or facial expression of your prospect.

Reminding yourself of your goal maintains focus on your ultimate objective. It is not your goal to impress your prospect with your vast knowledge about the product or service.

Rather, it is your purpose to help prospects make the best decision on their time for *their* reasons on *their* terms. With closing always on your mind, this requires that you learn by any means available what these times, reasons, and terms are.

How do you determine when to take the prospect to the next step?

The act of *trial closing* can play a huge roll in discovering if there is any basis for doing business now or later. It allows you to ascertain exactly where prospects stand.

Here are examples of trial closing questions (placed in the order of increasing obligation):
"John, are you with me so far?"
"Jane, are you following me?"
"Jim, does that make sense?"
"Bill, does that sound fair?"

As cited earlier, the manner in which questions are broached is emotionally neutral, inquisitive and non-presumptuous. The very nature of trial close questions is to test the water rather than persuade or close. Again, trial close questions are non-obligating and non-committal by design.

Stop, listen, think, and talk
The manner, tone, and attitude with which trial close questions are answered are much more revealing than the content of the answer.

If the tone, the enthusiasm or lack thereof, or any other tell-tale signal objectively observed is positive and if the prospect understands the value proposition, closing to the next step is *mandatory*. To do otherwise is tantamount to a disservice to the prospect you are pledged to help.

Not closing
Failing to close when the customer shows interest gives a mixed signal. They are telling you they are interested and you are demonstrating that they should not be interested. You are creating feelings of doubt and fear when you should be validating their feelings of interest.

It therefore does more harm than good to continue with the presentation after the customer has demonstrated interest. This is commonly referred to as *selling* to them and then buying it back.

A good rule of thumb is: Whenever in doubt, simply *ask* for the business. With certain prospects this is the only way to tell where they stand.

> "Many an election has been won or lost based solely on the fact that one candidate personally *asked* for more votes."
> —Anonymous

So much for the *why* and the *when…How* now do you close?

What makes a great close?
Other than appropriate timing, it is essential to identify the next step. It is akin to determining where you're going before you begin.

> **"If you don't know where you're going, you'll end up somewhere else"**
> **—Yogi Berra**

You need to always be closing toward a goal that is most comfortable for the prospect. This is essential to a well-built presentation flowing seamlessly into a positive response.

You never know if moving forward involves a consensus of decision makers/influencers or if you are talking to the final arbiter.

Starting at the top (Owner, CEO, President) and assuming others (consensus) are involved is always a safe bet initially.

Upon ascertaining the interests based on the responses to the trial closes the next question to ask is slightly more obligating or committal:

"How does it sound so far?"
"Does moving forward on this beginning to make sense?"
"Are all your questions answered?"

Types of Closes
There are hundreds of variations and combinations of fifteen basic closing categories.
These basic categories are as follows:
1. Direct question closes
2. Summary of three benefits closes
3. Paperwork closes
4. Impending event closes
5. Minor point closes
6. Yes momentum closes
7. Choice of two positives closes
8. Tie down questions
9. Boomerang closes
10. Story closes
11. Assumptive closes
12. "If-then" closes
13. Take away closes
14. Walkout closes
15. Consensus closes

Direct close:
This simple, direct question close presumes the combination of a strong relationship with unquestionable interest and motivation by the part of the final decision makers:

(Note: These are much more *obligating* questions used only with people ready to be closed)

Example:

"John, we have covered everything you need. Can you think of any reason we should *not* work together?"

Reply: "No, I can't."

You say, "All we need is the paperwork. Can we get that from you today?"

Alternate:
"John, it looks like you have all you need. This makes perfect sense, don't you think?" (Tie down question)

Reply: "Yes"

You: "All I need is the paperwork. Can I get that from you today?" (Assumptive)

Alternate:
You: John, this all makes sense, doesn't it?

Reply: "Yes."

You: "All I need now is to complete the paperwork. Can I get that from you today?"

Alternate:
You: "John, you're getting exactly what you want with this solution. You know it and you're even beginning to convince me. (Smile and pause.) All I need is your OK to try it. What do you think?"

Reply: "You may be right. I'll try it."

Note: It is not suggested that you jump up and down enthusiastically proclaiming, "Great, you've made a good decision!" This may remind the prospect-turned-buyer he went out on a limb and acted out of character. This could create doubt or buyer's remorse.
Instead, act confidently to congratulate rather than "thank" the buyer. Act professionally as if you always expected a "yes" response. Move seamlessly into the paperwork and/or consideration.

Summary close:
After paying close attention to the entire prospect's reactions (positive and negative), determine *three* hot buttons (benefits) that could have major impact on that prospect. Verbally list them all together followed by, "Does that sound about right? Or, Am I reading you correctly?"

Paperwork close:
An assumptive close that simply *starts* the process of filling out an application that must ultimately be completed to consummate the deal.

Impending event close:

"Joe, if we work together what would be your primary goal?"

Reply: "To increase sales in the next 90 days."

You (talk low, slow, and deliberately): "If you felt this would help you toward that 90-day goal could we move forward today?"

Reply: "Yes"

You: Use Direct close.

Minor point close:
Learn a single point of interest during the qualifying part of the cycle. Make that the major deciding factor.

You: "It certainly has a large kitchen, doesn't it?" (Tie down question)

Reply: "Yes it does"

You: "Does the kitchen have what you had in mind?"

Reply: "Yes"

You: "Would you change the color scheme or stay with this color?" (Choice of two positives)

Reply: "I like these colors"

You: "If we start the paperwork today you may be able to move in within thirty days…does that work with your schedule?" (Paperwork and impending event)

Yes momentum close:
This is simply a series of positive answer questions illustrated by the above example.

Choice of two positives:
See previous example

Tie down question:
This is a "leading question". An irrefutable statement with an almost rhetorical question tacked on. (Again, illustrated in the previous example)

Example:
"This would save a lot of money, wouldn't it?"

Boomerang close:
This is nothing more than answering a question with a question. This is commonly called *closing on resistance* (Jesus did this a great deal; politicians depend on this answer)

Example:
"*If* we could do that, then would you want to move forward right away?" (Like the "if-then" but used in answering an interested prospect's question)

Story close:
This close starts with, "Like I remember you saying…" and ends with, "Does that sound about right?" It uses information gathered in the QQP (Qualifying, questioning, and probing step in the cycle) creating a story in which the prospect is the lead character. It partially uses the same elements as the summary close.

Assumptive close:
Really this is part, to a greater or lesser degree, of most of the closes other than the "direct question" close.

Example:
"Jane, we appreciate your positive feedback. Is there anyone in particular you would want to work with on this?"
"Which options work best for you?"

Upon receiving a positive response go immediately to the Direct close.

"If – then close" This is the use of qualifying, pre-approach, and demo questions to lead to the close. This is often used in several other questions. More often than not, this close is used prior to the presentation in the QQP part of the sales cycle.

Example: "If we can get you what you want, then is this something you would want to move forward on right away?"

The Take-Away Close
If closing is characterized as a game of psychological warfare, the take-away is the secret weapon ju-jitsu move.

Properly deployed, this tactic can get things back on track for the genuinely interested prospect playing their emotional cards too close to their chests.

The take away is tantamount to calling the prospect's bluff while keeping the prospect's best interest at heart. Take-away techniques are highly individualized. One thing they have in common is a genuine attitude of resignation demonstrating no remorse or attitude while relying on the element of surprise.

Example:
Jerry (the prospect): "This is something we have needed to do for some time. I am just not sure the timing is right."

You (low, slow, sure): "Jerry, is that your only issue?"

Jerry: "Yes, that is the only thing."

You (do not pounce): "Jerry, if the timing was right you would definitely move forward?"

Jerry: "That's exactly right."

You (inquisitive): "Just out of curiosity, why would you?"

Jerry: "Well, like you said, I think it will save some time and money. Plus it may provide the competitive advantage we need."

You: "Jerry, I agree those are important however that may not enough to justify altering your time frame. Anyway, Jerry, it was certainly a pleasure getting to know you even though I was not able to help you get exactly what you need." (Break eye contact and start folding your tent displaying nothing that can possibly be perceived as disappointment.)

The objective here is to make the prospect feel good while you show that you do not feel badly. This unexpected move can, and often does, evoke an equally unexpected positive emotional countermove.

Jerry: "No, no, I didn't mean I didn't want to get it."

You: "Then, Jerry, can you think of any good reason we should not work together?"

Jerry: "No."

You: "Jerry, I look forward to serving you. We can make delivery in three weeks. Is that soon enough?"

Note: Using all the "war terminology" cannot and should not imply that you have an adversarial relationship with the prospective client. You are vowed to help. When the client wins, you win. The opposite is true as well.

Walk-out close:
This close is for smaller group final presentations:
You: "Is everyone with me? How does it sound so far?"

The reply is positive.

Example:
You: "Are their any final questions?"

The reply is "None."

You: "You have all the information you need to move forward. You have everything you need to draw a conclusion one way or another. (No pause.) I have to make a quick phone call (stand up and proceed to the door). If you will excuse me I will need just a few minutes. Why don't you all discuss it since you are together? I will be back to find out which way things are going. Is that fair enough?"
Note: By now you are out of the room.

(Wait 5 minutes or less well away from the door)

Upon your return: "Any additional questions or comments?"

If yes: Listen, think, and react to possible objections as questions leading to the close. Do not overreact. Everyone is watching.

If no: Go immediately and seamlessly into any variation of the **Direct close** aimed at the primary decision maker.

Typically, if a prospect demonstrates genuine interest and gives an objection it is an indication of interest. If this is the case you can close on the objection by use of a question.

Example:
Jane, "I think I like the proposal if we could do it after we finish XYZ."

You (stop, look, listen): "I know what you mean. When will XYZ start winding down?"

Reply: "In about 60 days." (Do not interrupt)

You: "If we could wait to start ramping up in 60 to 70 days, then could we complete the paperwork today?"

Reply: "I suppose so."

You: Use assumptive close (I.E. start writing)

Consensus Close
(Closing to the next step)
Sometimes the biggest mistake salespeople make is trying to close to the final step when they could have very easily closed to the *next* step. Trying to take too many steps at a time can cause you to stumble.

Next step
Often the next step is simply building a consensus. Here's how:

If the prospect answers in an unambiguous positive manner to a trial close (non-obligating) question, go seamlessly forward without breaking stride:

You: "John, here is what most (owners, CEOs, bakers, Indian Chiefs) *usually* do to move forward on this. First they *usually* want to check references. Then they *usually* want to have me explain the proposal to the others involved in moving forward."

There are no pauses between these sentences. The cadence of each of these declarative sentences is measured (slower) and deliberate. The attitude is extreme confidence. Each statement builds to an assumptive--but not presumptuous choice between something and something rather than something and nothing.

Example:

You: "Would you want to look at references or would you want someone else to look at them for you?" (Stop, look, listen. Encourage a response with no sign of impatience or interruption.)

If prospects are interested in the proposal it cannot be assumed that they enjoy or are confident in making decisions, especially by themselves. Additionally, it may be naïve to think the prospect is particularly astute in the decision-making department.

If the prospect replies in the affirmative continue by saying, "Who else, other than you, would be involved in moving forward?" Wait for a complete answer with no change in body language, demeanor, facial expression, or even breathing.

Take notes while inquiring what the positions and status of each of these decision makers/influencers are.

You: "Are Tom, Debra, or Elliot (name them using the notes just taken) here today?" Listen intently to the answer.

You: "Would there be a convenient time either today, tomorrow, or in a couple of days when we could get you and most of them (name them) together?" (Stop, look, listen, think, talk.) At this point pull out your appointment book or electronic calendar of choice and begin to write or type.

At this juncture you are inviting either agreement to the next step or an objection.

Closing is also an "attitude"
Stop, listen, think, show patient interest, do not react or answer until five (5) seconds after the prospect is completely finished talking.

Closing and decision-making can be traumatic for most people. A confident, matter-of-fact demeanor on the part of the salesperson counters doubts, fears and second-guessing on the prospect's part.

The proper use of tone, cadence or speed, and voice inflection are especially pertinent in the close. Read the following statements aloud, focusing only on the differences in meaning provided by each one:

"Here's what most people usually do."
"Here's what most people usually do?" (Is your tone throwing doubt what most people usually do?)

This is called turning the declarative into an interrogative. The difference in the message is like comparing lightning bolts and lightning bugs in helping people do what they love to do, that is, buy what they want or need.

What if you are absolutely convinced you are dealing with the one-and-only independent decision maker that needs no help, input, or validation from anyone else in the organization? First of all, this is as rare as the proverbial "hens' teeth." Prospects who volunteer they are the one-and-only are often not. They are not necessarily liars; they simply want to believe they are independent decision makers.

This individual may have previously decided "no" and has justified the negative decision to the others in the organization. In other words, they can only decide "no." It takes someone above them to decide in the affirmative.

Any salesperson can get a non-decision. It takes a professional to help a prospect arrive at an informed *yes* or *no*.

There are those who compare closing to fishing. Once you get a bite, and not just a nibble, you immediately and carefully, set the hook. If you wait a second too long to pull the opportunity is diminished. If you pull too fast the opportunity is thwarted by a lack of patience.

If you pull too hard you can break the line or take the hook along with the fish's lip.

Summary: Closing is the reason for selling. It is why you are there. It is absolutely the only way you can help people get what they want and/or need.

Personal Review: Would *you* buy from you? *Would* you buy from you? Would you *buy* from you? Would you buy from *you* if you didn't ask for the business in a timely, appropriate way?

Notes: _____

_____
_____
_____
_____
_____
_____
_____
_____

"This makes sense—this works—I can totally do this!"
—Anyone

CHAPTER EIGHTEEN
The Red Herring Dilemma

Objections may occur during any part of the sales cycle. As prospects become more sophisticated and more enlightened, they often start objecting from the very beginning. Typically, most objections come in the form of questions. Beware, however, not all questions are objections and not all objections are real.

Objecting is a natural human trait. Objections are part of any interested prospects buying rituals. When you are driving on the interstate and first notice that you need fuel, you probably do not immediately pull off at the very next service station. A buying ritual is in many ways akin to a behavioral pattern or habit. Whether you like to admit it or not, you are a creature of habit. (And most of us are slaves to our habits!)

When prospects are becoming sold, they will typically hedge their bets, thinking solely of intellectual reasons why they should not move forward.
Examples:
"It sounds good…I need to think about it"

"I need to check with someone else"

"I'll need to get back with you"

Sometimes these objections, or questions, are valid. However, typically they are **red herrings;** their purpose is to camouflage genuine feelings.

What is a "red herring"? It is a decoy, an excuse. There is no such thing as a "red herring" in nature. Treating an excuse as if were valid justifies their validity in the prospect's psyche.

Technically speaking an excuse is a lie with plausible deniability made by someone who wants to believe it as truth. Additionally, the person making the excuse wants you to believe it to be true.

> **"There are two reasons people do things, the real reason and the one that sounds real good."**
> **—J. Fred Landers**

Answers to objections don't work if the objection is simply part of a buying ritual, or a game on the part of the prospect. If the prospect is interested they will often give an excuse not to buy as a matter of course.

There are plenty of the good, logical answers to red herrings. Unfortunately, they do no good. After all, it does not matter how good your aim is when you're shooting at the decoy!

As mentioned earlier, by going for the decoy all you do is dignify the excuse giving it unwarranted credibility. Additionally, you set the tone for a debate you will always lose. If you win the argument, you lose the sale, and nobody wins.

What is a real objection and what is a red herring?
All red herrings sound real (they should since they are so well rehearsed).

There is a formula that works like magic. (**L.A.R.A.**)
- **L**isten empathetically without interruption and pause
- **A**gree respectfully and pause
- **R**epeat deliberately in the most unadulterated language and pause
- **A**sk if that's all, pause, and listen without preoccupation

You can now actually find the real objection! You have all the logical answers to all the objections prospects offer. If you fall for the ones that are not real and you go for the decoy, the prospect will always come up with more. In that case, no one wins

> **"There is often great disparity between what both the buyer and the seller *want* to believe, and what is actually true" —Me**

If you are convinced that what you hear, agreed to, and slowly repeat back as authentic, you cautiously and spontaneously respond:

You: "Joe, is there anything else (watch your tone)? Is that the only reason you would not move forward on this?" (Stop, look, listen, and pay careful attention to the prospect's tone.)

Prospect: "Yes."

Important note: Any inappropriate attitude or tone on your part can make this seem like a trick question setting a trap.

You are not competing with the prospect. You are not trying to win here. You can't. It is not your goal so it should not be your preoccupation. You are trying to help the prospect get what *he* wants.

You: "In other words, if it were not for that you would adopt this program right away?"(Really listen)

Caution: Speak softly, confidently and empathically. This is a moment of truth between parties. This is what separates those reasons that sound good, herrings of a crimson hue, from the bona fide reason.

Prospect: "Well . . ."

Congratulations, it took a lot of smoking out, but now you are about to hear the real reason. That so-called truth almost always comes down to money or value.

(Again, stop, look, and listen with no sign of interruption)

Go through L.A.R.A. (Listen, Agree, Repeat, Ask/Answer) this time changing the final **A** in L.A.R.A. to Answer.

Examples of answers to real objections for interested prospects fresh out of excuses:
If the objection is bogus or the prospect is not the final decision maker or if he or she is not sold or interested, a great answer is the last thing he or she needs to hear. It could even make the prospect mad!

The very old and reliable **Feel, Felt, Found** answer to most objections works like magic. It agrees, empathizes, cajoles, and offers a third party encouragement simultaneously.

Example:
"Jane, I know exactly where you're coming from. (**Feel**) You may be absolutely right. I may not have considered that. Let me ask you this. Hank Johnson of the Johnson Company (**good reference**) shared the same opinion (**felt**) way at first. As Hank Johnson thought about it, he began to realize (**found**) the value was far greater than the investment and the benefits would continue indefinitely."

Hint: To be agreeable, you must always agree and the word "but" cannot exist during any part of your presentation, especially when answering objections.

Shortcut: If you are sure the final objection comes down to money you can side-step the discovery (initial) L.A.R.A. scenario with:

"Jane, other than the money, is there any other factors that would prevent you from moving forward?"

Prospect: "No, not at all."

You (gently): "So if you could cost justify the value of the service we could complete the paperwork today?"

Prospect: "I think so, yes."

You (restate value proposition, use third party story if available): "The Johnson Company felt the same way at first. Hank Johnson agreed it costs him money, customers, and opportunity every day not to have this service in place. He adopted this concept because he felt it would save money, save time, and give his company a competitive edge. Does that make sense?"

Prospect: "That makes sense."

You: "All we need are a couple of pieces of paper to move forward. Can I get that from you today?"

Prospect: "I really believe this is the best thing for me to do both for myself and my company. How quickly can you start?"

You: "If we could start the training within the next three weeks could we wrap this up today?"

Prospect: "That will work just fine."

You: "Congratulations."

Understanding how to handle objections is more important than knowing all the answers. Please do not fall into the trap of taking excuses for reality. We have all done it and kicked ourselves (ouch!) afterward.

Summary: We are all human. We are all playing the game. Accept it and deal with it. Help the prospect move forward to get what she wants.

Personal Review: Would *you* buy from you? *Would* you buy from you? Would you *buy* from you? Would you buy from *you* if you answered all the red herrings and never got to the real reasons?

Notes:

"This makes sense—this works—I can totally do this!"
—Anyone

CHAPTER NINETEEN
Elevator Statements and Networking

We live in a world of sound bites and instant gratification. Today the *Gettysburg Address* would be considered epic.

Your strength here is in *brevity*. The majority of people have very short attention spans. They think seven times faster than you can talk. They jump to conclusions and form opinions quickly.

You can never know when you may have the opportunity to whet the appetite of a potential prospect or grab the interest over someone with influence.

"Be prepared" is not just the Boy Scout motto: It is good advice for anyone with a useful idea that can help others achieve their potential.

To be truly primed requires a sure-fire-never-miss thirty-second (or less) "commercial" that can be used at anytime and anywhere at the drop-of-a-hat.

For example, I have a very good attorney friend who started a business a few years back. Her elevator pitch for her business goes like this:

"Hi, I'm Tea Hoffmann, a lawyer and the founder of a company called Legal Training Group. We work with firms across the country, training them to become more efficient, effective, productive, and, ultimately, more profitable."

Her elevator speech seemed to say it all. Or at least it said everything that really needed to be said in less than forty words! The largest word she uses is productive, not exactly requiring a trip to Webster's!

One day at lunch she commented to me that her elevator pitch could be shorter. She could substitute E2/P2 in place of "…**e**fficient, **e**ffective, **p**roductive, and, ultimately, more **p**rofitable."

She said this would create curiosity which is one of the objectives of a great elevator pitch. I agreed.

A good elevator statement should:
- Be succinct and take less than thirty seconds (Tea's took fifteen seconds)
- Give the listener the impression that you are proud of your product, service, and/or company
- Provoke questions that could lead to a longer conversation
- Be memorable

A coherent, concise elevator speech will:
- Give you confidence
- Help focus your thoughts
- Assist you in building your prospecting network
- Improve the **branding** of your concept, company, product, or service

Professional personal selling requires constant thinking, creativity, and trusting your instincts. Trusting your instincts involves trying new ideas.

As mentioned previously, thinking about doing something without executing it is a form of procrastination caused by the diabolical nemesis known as *fear*.

Here are some critical concepts to keep steadfastly foremost in your mind.

Always be on alert for business opportunities. Every day take a little time to read local newspapers, trade journals and business journals to look for changes and opportunities in your industry. As you meet new people they ask what you do.

This "howdy-doody" time is not your cue to use the elevator statement. It is merely an opening to obtain pre-approach or qualifying information.

Wow-How Prospecting
How many times have you found yourself in a situation where someone asks you, "What do you do?" Lots!

This next illustration is a sure-fire way to spice up the conversation and at least get a referral *to* a referral if not a whole lot more!

Example:

You: "I make people rich and famous. What do you do?"

Suspect/Prospect: "I am the CEO of a growing mid-sized manufacturing."

You: "I have a *most unique* approach to sales"

Prospect: "What services do you provide?"

You: "Ted, I have been training, coaching, and creating successful sales tactics and strategies for over 40 years. Everything I do is customized and covers everything from the basics to advancing innovative new concepts. Maybe we should talk—even if only for future reference.

Ted: "Sounds good."

You: "Do you have your schedule handy?"

The object and the result of the *wow-how* elevator approach is to create curiosity and get either prospects or referrals by taking a different tact to answering the age old question we invariably and eventually get in various social settings,

Limit a good elevator or wow-how statement to twenty words in case it is only a two-story building. Now assume *all* buildings are only two stories.

Naturally, the illustration used here may be too good to be true. The question you should ask yourself out loud right now is, "Am I prepared when opportunity knocks?"

Never just do lunch
Lunch is not an excuse to eat. Lunch has to be prepared for with goals, objectives, and questions. Do not make lunch too structured. But do not waste time in small talk.

Make sure you control the lunch meeting:
- Make it convenient to the guest. Pick up the prospect if you can. Wash the car inside and out first.
- Position yourself with your back to the wall so the guest will not be distracted.
- Order easy to eat, affordable food. Big leafy salads are often labor intensive, awkward and messy.
- Use your best table manners. Check a book of etiquette if you can't recall which side the drink, bread, knife or fork should reside.
- Do not drink alcohol when discussing business even if the prospect does.
- Be considerate of the other person's time and stay on schedule.
- Follow-up with a personal e-mail (ask permission to use the prospect's e-mail). A hand-written thank-you note is always best although not always feasible.

The effective use of business cards
Use business cards wisely. Do not treat the exchange of business cards as automatic and matter-of-fact. Ask for everyone else's business cards. You make others feel important by the way you treat their business card. Always give 2 business cards. It's twice as good as one.

Look closely at cards and comment on any new or noteworthy information. Hand prospects two business cards and point out information you want to draw to their attention.

Keep all information organized electronically (ACT, Goldmine, Blackberry, etc) for use in follow-up.

Summary: Modern elevators travel fast so be brief.

Personal Review: Why would *you* buy from you? *Would* you buy from you? Would you *buy* from you? Would you buy from *you* if you never took advantage of the opportunity?

Notes:

"This makes sense—this works—I can totally do this!"
—Anyone

CHAPTER TWENTY
Communicating Clear Value Propositions (VP)

When you think of value go back to the basic fundamentals. All products and services are the same, commoditized, except for differences in value. These so-called "differences" need not be tangible or extraordinary. However, they must be communicated and perceived because perception is reality.

That is why every business or organization must develop and promote a unique value proposition (VP). Usually no more than three characterizations used to create a unique perception.

Notice that I did not say or even imply that they were actually unique. Everyone claims to offer everything else that their competitors do. But I'm not saying that they were *not* unique. That is not the point. The actual competition is between perceptions, not realities.

The only constant in an effective value proposition is that it be compelling enough (emotion vs. logic, passion vs. pragmatism) to stand up against price. In a society where price is allowed to become more important than value, value will cease to exist, as it did in the USSR during the cold war.

Value is the primary bi-product of salesmanship in the free enterprise system. Value and perception must be sold! A great VP is the "trump card" of a winning presentation and close, and it makes handling objections much less problematic.

Determining this magic value proposition that differentiates you from all others begins with four questions:

1. Who is the competition?
2. How good are they at getting their message across?
3. What is the target market?
4. What is unique about the company or the product that better appeals to the target than the competition?

Without first determining the answers to these questions, it would be like having surgery without a proper diagnosis. Amputating when an antibiotic would more appropriate prevents the adverse long-range consequence.

What do you do when you have gotten their attention?
Once you define the competition and the target market, you are left with both an opportunity and a challenge.

What makes you, your company, or your product/service unique? Use this test during brainstorming. Say whatever comes to mind and immediately ask yourself these questions:

1. Can the competition also say that?
2. Is the competition saying that?
3. Are they getting their message across?
4. Why would that make me different?
5. How important is that to the target market and how would the prospect react to it?

Objective answers to these questions will yield the one, two, or three unique values necessary to build a value proposition.

> **To be successful in business, you must be unique. You must be so different, that if people want what you have, they must come to you to get it." —Walt Disney**

It has been said many times by many sales trainers that the only antidote to price shock is value. Yet this is a gross understatement. While people talk price, they cannot live without value.

Finding the magic words to clearly define value in the prospects' terms in their words and thinking is essential to your ultimate goal which is, of course, helping people buy what they want and need today.

Analytical
If the buyer is analytical (a thinker), a cost analysis may be in order. Always allow the prospect to do the math or he will believe that you are trying to pull something over on him.

Example:
You: "Jane, you can especially appreciate this. We are working with Hank Johnson—whom I believe you know. He crunched some figures that may make sense in your situation. Got a pencil? Please jot this down if you don't mind. Your figures show this will save about $100K over 3 years. Do these figures jive reasonably with your estimates? Are you sure these are conservative enough?"

Prospect: "Our figures agree and I think they are very realistic."

You: "The total investment including everything on our part and your work would be less than $22.5K per year. Do these figures work in your thinking?"

Prospect: "I can agree with them."

You: "Jane, would you consider moving forward based on **your** figures?"

Prospect: "Does it come in blue?" (An inside sales joke)

Prospects may not always believe what you say, however they always believe what *they* say!

Value
Prospects buy today based on their perception of value. Tomorrow this prospect will help you help their friends do likewise. This is the most effective and efficient way to sell.

Here are the top ten generic value propositions:
- Save money
- Save time
- Solve a problem
- Ease a pain
- Provide an advantage
- Increase profits
- Make job easier
- Keep up with the competition
- Look good to their customers, employees, board, spouse, God
- Any combination of the above will work just as well.

Summary: Try everything. See what works. Keep it brief. Keep it simple. Implement – test – revise – learn. Use it all the time.

Personal Review: Would *you* buy from you? *Would* you buy from you? Would you *buy* from you? Would you buy from *you* if you did not see the value in doing so?

Notes: _____

_____
_____
_____
_____
_____
_____
_____
_____

"*This makes sense—this works—I can totally do this!*"
—Anyone

CHAPTER TWENTY-ONE
Goals, Planning, Accountability, and the Law of Averages

People are not plants. Unlike vegetables, humans cannot grow without goals, planning, accountability and a healthy respect for the law of averages.

While it sounds melodramatic, virtually everything a person will ever accomplish begins with a goal, an objective, a vision or a purpose. Every plan ever implemented started with a well-defined goal.

It is impossible to overstate the importance of clear and written goals. Focusing on a goal provides energy!

> **"A goal is more than a dream; it is a dream being acted upon."**
> **—David J. Schwartz, Ph.D.**

In the world of personal sales, the roles of goal setting and planning are critical. This can be explained by the voluntary masochism of proactively exposing yourself to rejection, not to mention the many other frustrating and demeaning acts that are the hallmark of personal sales. This is why you have the opportunity to earn big bucks!

The more difficult or important the task the more crucial it is that you begin with detailed, written goals coupled with deadlines you can plan around.

Declaring, "I'm going to sell as much as I can!" is not a goal. Rather, it is a death wish, a fool's folly, a dreamer's dream.

> **"A man without a goal is like a ship without a rudder."**
> **—Benjamin Franklin**

So how do you set a real goal?

Ask yourself how you picture yourself five or even ten years from now. How much money will that require allowing for inflation and emergencies? Divide it by the number of months involved. Factor in some ramp-up time. Now you have a monthly goal. Is it challenging enough? Is it realistic? Are you committed to it? Three yes's and you are on your way!

A goal without a plan is a pipedream
Here's the good part. Break down your goal into average days per month, taking into account industry norms and holidays. Make sure there is balance in your life. Take into account family, social, spiritual, and recreational time.

> **"How do you eat an elephant? One bite at a time! (Same way you eat a cow)"—Anonymous**

Now that you have things broken down into days let's take it one step further.

Break that workday into thirds (8AM-11AM, 11AM-2PM, 2PM-5PM). What would you need to accomplish every third of every business day to accomplish your five-or ten-year goal?

In personal sales, a result may be defined several different ways, depending on the larger goal and time frame involved.

Examples of sales results:
- Setting appointments with existing clients for referrals
- Calling referrals to get appointments
- Meeting with clients to talk about referrals
- Presenting or closing sales
- Meeting referrals to begin a presentation (a relationship)
- Following up to get to the next step

Anything other than these activities needs to be done outside the one-third day sales time.
- Preparation
- Training
- Administration
- Straightening our desk
- Your life

> **"Success by the yard is hard; but by the inch, a cinch!"**
> **—Earl Nightingale**

Remember fifty per cent of your productive phone contacts come before 8:30 AM and after 4:30 PM. Those are the times when the gatekeeper is not on duty and the decision maker may pick up the phone.

Prepare the night before. Indulge in on-the-job (OTJ) training all the time, while reading, CD's, phone coaching for evenings, early mornings, and weekends. Administration and organization are relegated to before 7:30 AM and after 5:30 PM.

If you work it easy, it's hard. If you work it hard, it's easy.

It takes twenty-one days to form a habit. How strong are habits? Say "no" while shaking your head "yes." Say "yes" while shaking your head "no." Cross your arms the Direct way. Now uncross and try the opposite way.

It is hard to break a bad habit and it is equally challenging to break a good one. Creating good habits is difficult. Living with bad habits is worse.

> **"If your goal is nothing you will surely reach it!"**
> **—Charles Jones**

Once you have gotten into efficient, effective routine committed to worthwhile goals, it is time for you to deal with the long arm of the LAW. Which law?

The law that rules the sales universe is reverently known as the law of averages.

According to this mysterious law of averages you can do everything exactly right and fall flat on your face. This is how you learn most of life's most important lessons. The first life lesson is how to get up when you most feel like throwing in the towel. This is the stuff that defines character, that intangible element that will ultimately have more to do with who you are and what you accomplish than all the information you learn and people you know.

> **"The greatest glory is not in never falling but in rising up every time we fall."—Confucius**

Even when the product or service is valid and timely (and not that disruptive) and you are working hard and smart things may not progress as planned. The LAW is always working so it is that more vital you maintain a positive mental attitude. Results will come with patience when you truly believe in the LAW.

Is the LAW then working against you when things are going very well? You would think so in a logical universe. This is the great paradox of the LAW. You function in a dynamic world where the physics of inertia works in your favor. When things are going well and you allow us to believe, success does indeed breed success. Then self-confidence kicks in like a rush of adrenaline.

> **"People don't plan to fail, they just fail to plan."**
> **—Emerson**

When your goals and your plans get into gear
When you are committed to a worthy goal some extraordinary elements become unleashed. It has been said that committed worthy goals can take over the subconscious and keep a person going in the right direction.

When goals become positive obsessions, it is like being equipped with an automatic pilot. Hurdles previously causing insurmountable consternation do not even require a second thought. Blinders keep out doubts, fears, and previous frustrations.

When you fully acquiesce to goals, you allow your subconscious brain signals to instinctively tell you what to do and what to avoid.

"The goal constantly speaks, 'I am the image you want to make real. Here is what you must do to make me real'."
—David J. Schwartz, Ph.D., *the Magic of Thinking Big*

Summary: Plan your work and work your plan. People don't plan to fail, they fail to plan.

Personal Review: Would **you** buy from you? **Would** you buy from you? Why would you **buy** from you? Would you buy from **you** if you gave up too soon? Would you respect you if you did not appear to have a well thought-out plan?

Notes:
___

"This makes sense—this works—I can totally do this!"
—Anyone

CHAPTER TWENTY-TWO
The 800-Pound Gorilla

There is an 800-pound gorilla in the room and it seems like the personal sales industry is trying to ignore it. This "persona non gratis" is follow-up.

My research and experience unearthed a huge disconnect between the supply and demand for follow-up information properly field tested and proven to work.

Most closings in the professional world of sales are not the slam-bang-thank-you variety. One-call closes do occur, but they are rarer in many industries. The sales cycles more often require two, three or more personal contacts sometimes lasting up to a year or more.

As I surf the Internet and visit bookstores on the subject of follow-up, I find copious amounts of follow-up letters with little else on the in's and out's of effective follow-up know-how.

How to love 'em and leave 'em and get them to buy
Leaving the prospect without getting a decision can be precarious. Analytical buyers, buyers dependent upon a consensus, and buyers requiring a certain amount of due-diligence before they can move forward requiring additional contacts or meetings is a fact of life.

Determining the motives behind the procrastination is the dilemma you always face.

Follow-up letters have their place
There is nothing better than a handwritten follow-up letter to thank someone for his business, remind him of an upcoming meeting, or to reiterate or drive an important point home.

Yet with the advent of e-mail, "snail mail" is quickly becoming a thing of the past. How can you use e-mail without losing the advantage of the written or typed word?

The answer is to talk about it with the prospect. Learn how the person feels and what kind to correspondence he or she prefers and proceed accordingly.

Embrace technology
Depending on the industry, there is a load of information to maintain in order to be efficient and organized. There are many efficient ways to do this with the technologies available today.

Prospect lists, databases, scheduling and follow up can be tracked effectively using any of dozens of readily available software programs.

The key is to make sure the technology works for you and is consistent with the rest of your organization. The danger is these new found timesavers are an excellent source for creative avoidance.

Why follow-up at all?
Hopefully, at this point, it is self-evident. You serve at your prospects' pleasure and in their time constraints. Trying for some kind of shortcut or appearing the least bit impatient or disappointed can prolong or stall the closing process. One of the most common reasons for a slowdown in the commitment process is that the prospect does not feel he is winning. The prospect has not convinced him or her, with your help, of any sense of urgency.

A major purpose of the first meeting is to get the process on track and in place to move toward. The process may well be to set up that second group meeting to form a consensus.

You do the Direct closes and the walk-out, and it is evident the decision maker is very interested, but would lose face with his group if you leaned any harder and he acquiesced.

A good time to go fishing
I'm referring to commitment fishing.

Example:
You: "John, just out of curiosity, we seem to have covered everything with everyone involved. What factors are you considering in becoming part in this program?"

John: "Nothing else really. I just need time to think about it."

You: (stoically, patiently) "John. I know exactly where you are coming from. Have you been able to realize the value of the proposal?"

John: "Yes, I just need time to think."

A commitment to a commitment
You (stoically without interrupting): "John, that is perfectly understandable. What would be a reasonable amount of time that would be needed for you to move one way or another?"

John: "Two days should be plenty."

You (stoically, empathetically): "John, considering all you need to think about are you sure two days will be enough time?"

This is a bit of a "take-away" close. It both demonstrates patience and lack of anxiety. Your attitude must still be emotionally tuned in to ask this question effectively.

John: "I think that will be plenty."

You: "Let me ask you this, John. Where will you be on Thursday? (Two days hence) The reason I ask is I may be in the area and able to drop in. Otherwise, I will just call. Anyway, it's just a thought."

John: "I will just getting back in town. Maybe some time in the late afternoon."

You: "I will call first. Something could come up. Let's tentatively plan on three o'clock. Does that work for you? (Pause) Why don't I call you tomorrow when I know more?"

John: "All right."
At this point you are trying to get a commitment to the commitment.

One day later...
Speaking to the gatekeeper with whom you should have a good relationship by now:

You: "Suzie, is John in? He is expecting my call."

John: "Hello."

You: (enthusiastically) "I started to call you this morning, but I thought better of it. The reason I wanted to call is, late yesterday afternoon I got some good news and new information on the program we discussed, but it can keep until Thursday. I can be there by three. Are we still on track?"

John: "Sure, I will see you then."

Note: Keep a going list of good news and new information on hand at all times. Examples include new customers, customer comments, customer results, or features and benefits not previously mentioned.

This is always your ulterior motive for getting together with truly hot prospects to **go to the next step or wrap things up.** Naturally, the real reason for the meeting is to wrap things up and come to a conclusion one way or another. You know it and they certainly know it.

When Jack Nicholson said, "You can't handle the truth!" in the 1990's movie "A Few Good Men", he was speaking of a reality that has much more application to sales than meets the eye. It is the *sound* of the unmitigated truth that people have an emotional problem with.
Don't the words "try it" for all practical purposes mean "start doing it?" When the prospect says, "let me think about it" doesn't it really mean stop thinking about it?

Proper follow-up requires an imprecise element called "pleasant persistence." When trying to decide how much is too much, simply apply the golden rule.

"Nothing in the world can take the place of persistence. Talent will not; nothing is more common than unsuccessful men with talent. Genius will not; unrewarded genius is almost a proverb. Education will not; the world is full of educated derelicts. Persistence and determination alone are omnipotent. The slogan 'Press On' has solved and always will solve the problems of the human race."
—Calvin Coolidge

Summary: Demonstrate to the prospect that there is no question about the fact that you care. Don't give up on serving the reluctant prospect. They need us most!

Personal Review: Why would *you* buy from you? *Would* you buy from you? Would you *buy* from you? Would you buy from *you* if you dropped the ball?

Notes:

"This makes sense—this works—I can totally do this!"
—**Anyone**

CHAPTER TWENTY-THREE
Why Don't All Interested Prospects Buy?

You know your stuff. You have done your homework. All the building blocks are stacked efficiently and effectively. You presented. You trial closed. The prospect showed interest and you went seamlessly and confidently into a well-planned close. You handled the objection and the prospect agreed with your value proposition.

So why didn't the prospect buy? Why do some prospects buy while others do not?

Sometimes people buy because you just catch them at the right time, the right place and in the right mood. It can and does happen. Nevertheless, this is more often *not* the case. Is there any upside to cooling your jets and wait to take orders from the motivated prospects? Waiting on the proverbial and unpredictable *bluebird* of happiness to land in your lap is wholly unrealistic.

What about timing?
Timing is overrated. While it certainly is important it is not *everything*.

Perfect timing then is especially overrated. If you depend on the alignment of the moon, you will miss all the opportunities life has for you.

The more you see, the more you learn. The more you fail, the more you will inevitably succeed. "Just do it" is more than an advertising slogan; it is the imperative for living.

Prospects buy because they are given the best opportunity to buy. Millions of products and services never see the light of day because nobody tried to properly sell them. The salespeople must have been waiting until it was convenient or felt right. Guess what? The time will never feel perfectly right. *Action* precedes feeling, not the other way around.

"*Just do it* is more than just a pithy ad campaign. It can be a life long habit that makes all the difference as we look back over what we accomplished in our time on earth."
—Anonymous

"The credit belongs to the man who is actually in the arena, whose face is marred by dust and sweat and blood…who knows the great enthusiasms; who spends himself in a worthy cause; who at best in the end knows the triumph of high achievement. And…if he fails, at least fails while daring greatly, so his place will never be with those cold and timid souls who know neither victory nor defeat."
—Theodore Roosevelt

Selling is more *art* than science.
By far, the number one reason prospects inexplicably don't buy is because they are not yet sold. The prospect does not understand, appreciate, or relate to the features, benefits, or value proposition of what has been presented.

Most of the chapters in this book address one facet or another that, even if executed perfectly and cohesively, cannot and will not guarantee a particular prospect will buy.

This is the reason selling has worth. This is why top performers skilled and disciplined in the use of superlative tools and tactics are of highest value in our economic system.

After any given sales call, you can only make an educated guess about what went wrong or what could have been done differently.

Luck of the draw
Sales cycles vary from industry to industry and from person to person. Notwithstanding all the magic motivational words of tested, tried and true sales methodology, often the success rate comes down to old-fashioned persistence and the law of averages.

The objective is to get a *yes* or *no* answer
Only in the world of academia can 1+1 always equal a predictable sum.

Sometimes, despite skillfully attaining attention, cultivate interesting and evoke desiring of the qualified, referred, prospect you only increase the odds. Nothing in personal sales is automatic or predictable. You are at best sticking out your neck, exposing yourself to possible failure and rejection.

Let's assume you do not allow yourself to fall in the trap of over-selling. If you get a positive answer to a trial close question early you most certainly can increase your chances of serving the prospect.

Let's consider this hypothetical…what if you:

- Give a compelling presentation
- Express a convincing value proposition
- Close when there is interest
- Handle interested objections
- Then you further enhance the opportunity to help the prospect do what the prospects love to do, which is buy.

You do everything right—would you buy? Would you always buy from you? Sometimes you would—and sometimes you would not. The question is unanswerable. This is where character and a positive attitude resolve are tested.

There could be a number of competitive factors, personal reasons, or fears. Remember that these are interactions between human beings. At best, the sales dynamic is unpredictable.

You can only do your best while always believing that your best is good enough. It may sound hokey—nevertheless, when your reach exceeds your grasp, your best just gets better! *This* is always the paramount time for learning.

> "Victory is not final—defeat is not fatal—the most important thing is courage."
> —Winston Churchill

> **"In every seeming adversity there is a seed of greater benefit."–Sam Johnson**

You can control what you can control and nothing more.

You can write down your goals, form good habits, study, learn, and implement your plan on schedule, all the time maintaining your enthusiasm. (Nothing great was ever done *without* enthusiasm.)

Disruptive innovation (disruptive technology)
The term "disruptive technology" was coined by a Harvard Business School professor, Clayton Christensen, in 1998. It applies to new ideas or concepts that require a change in beliefs and thinking that may threaten someone's income, their power, their job, or the way they perceive themselves. Selling even the best of ideas that are against the *status quo* is "disruptive".

Why am I mentioning this here? Because sometimes (too often) an otherwise very proficient sales person cannot understand why everything goes so right in the sales process— why every part of the sale is perfectly in sequence— from the initial contact to the trial close of a perfectly compact presentation to a close at the peak of interest— however the seeming prime prospect could not be moved no matter what. The problem is this. Let's say you have an absolute cure for all disease on earth. Who would believe it and who could possibly buy? Think about it.

The axiomatic rule of human nature is, "people can only believe what they *want* to believe. They only want to believe what they can afford to believe; they only do what they *have* to do only *when* they have to do it.

Disruptive concepts go against human nature. No doctor, no hospital administrator, no nurse, no lab technician, and no hospital janitor, in accordance with human nature, can afford to believe you have a cure for all disease!

Does this mean we in the sales profession don't think it worth the effort, the frustration, and the potential rejection to promote what we are convinced is true?

> **"Success consists of going from failure to failure without loss of enthusiasm."**
> **—Winston Churchill**

Is life fair? No. It never was, it was never meant to be, and it will likely *never* be. Yes, you can do many things to help level the playing field. Nonetheless the law of averages is absolutely irrevocable. However, the harder you work, think, and apply what you learn the luckier you get! And the more confidence you gain.

That guarantee is made every day by that person staring back at you in the mirror.

There are a variety of ways to address the basic principles of selling
Personal selling can be both very rewarding and challenging at the same time.

Many neophytes lose perspective right away. Subsequently, they allow themselves to become overly discouraged. During the first few months, a large percentage of them give up. They concentrate far more on results than on the thinking, attitude, study, activities, and habits that cause results. They slide into a comfortable rut and lose sight of what they are trying to accomplish for their prospects and themselves.

If you don't want that to happen, concentrate on these basics:

Take the tools and tactics *one at a time*.

Anything giving you the feeling, "This makes sense—this works— I can totally do this!" should take priority. Internalize the new idea or tactic until it becomes natural. Revise it to fit your individual personality until you are confident and comfortable.

You can never allow yourself to stop learning. Life is continuous. Success is a journey, not a destination. Focus only on what you can control.

> **"If we know it all – we have a lot to learn."**
> **—A Church Marquee on Hillsboro Road near Franklin, Tennessee**

You will always love the sales profession in direct proportion to how well you adapt to the job. Our happiness with selling is inexplicably tied to our proficiency in the basics and our ability to motivate ourselves to improve.

Do yourself a favor. Do the world a good deed. Keep a promise to yourself to never stop raising your goals and perfecting your skills and...*above all*—Stop selling! Let 'em buy.

Summary: Give the prospects your best. Let them decide for themselves. And as always, keep the faith.

Personal Review: Would *you* buy from you? *Would* you buy from you? Would you *buy* from you? Would you buy from *you*? **It all depends on you!**

Final Review: The world of business is dramatically changing. The byproducts of dynamic change are resistance and confusion. Excellence in personal sales can be the antidote to misunderstanding. Increased proficiency in sales is a key to overcoming resistance through trust.

Notes:

After Thought

This chapter is not in the Table of Contents. This is my first book and I have attempted to cover forty years of experience.

I would like to think I not only paid my dues but also *paid attention* during that time. I took copious notes and tried my best to practice each idea in a variety of real life sales situations in which the success of my company, my livelihood, and my reputation depended not only on the results but also my ability to learn so I could teach others with greater or lesser God-given talents and formal education to use with "confident competence".

If you are a very discerning reader you discerned early on that I penned every word in this book myself. I did this because I believed the content would have more credibility if it appeared (actually was) "first hand" based on personal knowledge and experience.

I enjoyed every hour put into this book. I hope and pray it provided value for you, you will communicate by email with me, and you will encourage others to invest in my book (or books) and/or training if you are so led.

If you have a sales organization or if you are around others whose lives are directly effected by their better understanding the principles contained in this book, I invite you to contact me about speaking and/or volume discounts.

"This really does make sense—this really does work—you can totally do this!"
—Anyone

The rest is up to *you*— so what's the next step?
Are you proactively improving your sales skills? The cost of improving is *pennies* on every dollar lost by *not* improving. Think about it. Maybe you don't need an overhaul –maybe just a tune-up!

These listed services are designed to help unearth root causes of potential personal sales issues and provide cost-effective solutions. Do this now to make you and/or your company more efficient, effective, productive, and profitable. (Great value at great rates)
1. One-hour workshops on any chapter in the book. Select any relevant chapter
2. 2- day sales "tune ups" for yourself and/or your organization
3. Individual field analysis. Two days shadowing one salesperson with diagnosis, analysis, and a report
4. Sales management analysis. Four days shadowing one sales manager with diagnosis, analysis, and report
5. Sales structure, monitoring, reporting, schedules, goals, and quotas. Two days with comprehensive strategy session
6. One-day basic training classes. Choose 4 chapters.
7. Coaching customized to individual goals. (weekly/monthly)
8. Customized approaches, presentations, closes, answers to objections. Two-week turn around
9. Competitive analysis – value proposition and product differentiation. One-day session

Remember, an investment made in *you* has no downside with unlimited *upside* potential and every minute wasted is lost forever.

Contact:
Chuck Blackburn
chuck@chuckblackburnonline.com
www.stopsellingletembuy.com
Brentwood, Tennessee
615-330-2302

Your thoughts, comments, reflections, notes:

Please email me at chuck@chuckblackburnonline.com or chuck@stopsellingletembuy.com with your comments. Thank you.

Made in the USA